LIFE's
alphabet
SOUP

WHEN YOUR CHILDREN
MAKE YOU EAT YOUR WORDS

Other books by Terri Ferran

Finding Faith
Having Hope

that meant that they wouldn't have to do the yard work at all.

When they discovered the truth, they made sure we knew that there is only one thing worse than being forced to do yard work to earn your spending money, and that is to be forced to do yard work and not get paid for it at all. Suddenly they were urging me to work part-time, at least.

Being the equitable parents that we are, we offered to split up the yard work duties, including Mom and Dad in the rotation, but they still grumbled. I can't prove it, but I'm pretty sure they prayed for drought.

The real blow landed when we announced that, after reviewing our budget, we needed to adjust their allowance amounts. Down, not up. The sixteen-year-old didn't care because what would have been his allowance already went to pay for his half of the auto insurance. The thirteen-year-old's pay cut didn't matter as much because when we switched houses she would be "moving away from all of her friends and wouldn't have anything to spend money on anyway!" (drama slightly added).

Our ten-year-old son was sorely disappointed. Just when his allowance was due to be raised, the rules changed. Although we pointed out that we weren't actually cutting his allowance, like we did his sister's, he had already been planning on the glorious day when he would have double the money to spend. He rivaled a teenager with the depth and breadth of his suffering sighs and hints about how much better life would be if I just went back to work.

The seven-year-old whined a little, but we reminded her that she would still have enough to buy fake fingernails (that never stayed on for long) from the dollar store once a month, and she would still be able to buy candy here and there. That child just needed a beauty and candy fix periodically, and she was fine.

When the resistance to allowance cuts got too intense, we could (and did) remind them that we didn't have to pay any allowance at all. I also thought I might have to remind them I could still afford soap to wash away those nasty words they muttered.

In our house, allowances weren't directly tied to chores, but were given to each child as a method for teaching money management skills. Based on their age, each was given a certain amount of "pay" each payday for their own use.

Not being the most original people, we borrowed an idea from some friends. We took six Ziploc bags and a shoebox for each child. The bags were labeled "Long-term savings," "Personal savings," "Charitable contributions," "Birthday," "Christmas," and "Spending."

Into each of the first five bags went ten percent of their pay. If their pay was ten dollars, a dollar went into every bag, except the "Spending" bag which got the remaining fifty percent.

This method taught them several things (including to always check shoeboxes for money). Their long-term savings were earmarked for college, service missions, or car payments, and were deposited into a savings account periodically. The personal savings were for special items they really wanted and could save for, such as a bike, scooter, stereo, mp3 player, and so on. The charitable contributions taught them to give to others.

LIFE's
alphabet
SOUP

WHEN YOUR CHILDREN
MAKE YOU EAT YOUR WORDS

Terri Ferran

CFI
Springville, Utah

ISBN 13: 978-1-59955-286-6

Published by CFI, an imprint of Cedar Fort, Inc., 2373 W. 700 S., Springville, UT 84663
Distributed by Cedar Fort, Inc. www.cedarfort.com

LIBRARY OF CONGRESS CATALOGING-IN-PUBLICATION DATA

Ferran, Terri, 1962-
  Life's alphabet soup : when your children make you eat your words / Terri
Ferran.
    p. cm.
  ISBN 978-1-59955-286-6 (acid-free paper)
  1. Motherhood--Humor. 2. Mothers--Humor. 3. Families--Humor. I. Title.

PN6231.M68F47 2010
814'.6--dc22

                        2009009058

Cover design by Angela D. Olsen
Cover design © 2010 by Lyle Mortimer
Edited and typeset by Heidi Doxey

Printed in Canada

10 9 8 7 6 5 4 3 2 1

Printed on acid-free paper

To Brianna, Joey, Skyler, Chantelle, DJ, & Savannah

Without you I wouldn't be a mother. I would have much more money, much less happiness, and this book would be listed under fiction. Keep being you—I'm taking notes.

Contents

CONTENTS

Preface

Before You Get to the Alphabet

I have been "gainfully" employed from the time I was thirteen years old, which means I have worked for a paycheck, either full- or part-time (mostly full-time) for over thirty years. I've been "painfully" employed for a good part of that time. When I started my working career, I made $1.10 per hour. When I quit, I was making a six-figure income.

I was successful. I was a woman who had it all. For me, "all" included a loving, understanding husband, six children (with a "No More Pets" contract signed by them), a beautiful home, a challenging career as a CFO, and fulfilling volunteer work at my church. "All" also included Fibromyalgia Syndrome and Major Clinical Depression.

The day finally dawned when I gave my notice at work, and I felt an unbelievable lightening of my load.

My job was demanding and stressful. For years I loved the positive strokes I got from it, not to mention the paycheck. I juggled the demands of career and family with the kind of Herculean strength I believed only women possessed.

I struggled through the years when my children were

• • • IX • • •

young, trying to find adequate day care, envying those co-workers who had mothers, grandmothers, or aunts to help them. In that regard, I was on my own.

I made it through the early years, blessed by the fact that my three oldest children were self-motivated, independent creatures. When I was overcome by the guilt of leaving them to latch-key, they often reassured me that they were fine; and, like me, they were not willing to pay the price of giving up the paycheck if I stayed at home with them.

Eventually we adopted three more children, and we were determined to give them a better chance at life than they were born with. It was then that we learned determination only goes so far before reality sets in.

In my case, reality hit me upside my head when I had to face the fact that I just couldn't do it all. With the help of a counselor and my physician, I was diagnosed as being clinically depressed (a blow magnified by the fact that, up to that point, I just didn't believe in clinical depression). I was also diagnosed with Fibromyalgia Syndrome (FMS). Even with those diagnoses, it took several more years before I was compelled to admit to myself that I wasn't—and more importantly didn't have to be—"Super Woman."

Am I an expert mom? Like most women, I have had to become an expert at managing my own life, and like most women, I do have something to share. When we realize that where we are may not be where we want to be, then we can begin to change it.

Sometimes life takes faith and prayer, and sometimes you just have to laugh and find the humor in it.

This book won't solve your problems, but maybe it will help you see them in a different light. And by shedding new light on your problems, I hope this book will make you chuckle and make your load feel just a little less heavy.

A special thanks goes to Dr. Seuss, whose books helped me make it through my life rife with strife as a mother and wife. I especially love his ABC book, which I have memorized and tried hard not to plagiarize!

Allowance . . .

Big A, Little A,
What begins with A?
Allowance! Mom, if you quit work,
Will it affect my pay?

There are some questions in life that just can't be answered properly until you experience them for yourself. For instance, which is more painful—a root canal or a poke in the eye with a sharp stick? I can tell you from experience that a root canal is better than a poke in the eye with a sharp stick. But that is another story for another day.

A choice you're more likely to face is: Which is more painful—going from two paychecks to one or listening to your children whine about how poor you are? Again, I speak from experience, but not very coherently or decisively. Both options can break you.

When I quit work, I was stressed about how we would cope when the LOM (Lack of Money) hit. Although my husband made a pretty good living, our income was cut by more than half when I quit my perfectly good job to stay at home. The stress was compounded by the fact that we had just paid thousands for landscaping the home we could no longer afford to stay in once I quit working.

We sold our dream home, moved to a smaller house, and informed the children that we wouldn't be able to foot the bill for their college. The two older ones had moved out by then, and my oldest daughter had her college degree, so she didn't really care. My second oldest had squandered his "free ride" at college on major party time and was on his own at that point anyway.

Our third child took it rather hard, because he remembered the Disneyland/Cancun years much better than the youngest three. In true sixteen-year-old fashion, he mourned the passing of the Corvette, which we sold just as he finally got his license. He made sure we heard his opinion on the subject. He had been ripped off—first, no college education; and second, the Corvette, which had been left to him in our wills, was sold out from under him. It didn't seem to matter to him that we would have had to actually die for him to benefit from that whimsical provision; for him, it was the principle of the thing. I was glad he knew what principles were, but I wasn't as enthusiastic about the fact that this one involved my death.

The three youngest were, at first, supportive of my decision to stay at home. Still forced to attend their middle school/grade school torture chambers, they had no desire to go to college.

We explained my health problems to them, and they claimed they wanted me to feel better. But what really perked them up was when they heard we could no longer afford to pay them to do the yard work for us. They mistakenly assumed

And the birthday money provided a fund they could use to purchase a present for a sibling or a friend, though we did have to watch a couple of children who thought they should buy birthday presents for themselves. The Christmas bag assured them that there would be money for Christmas shopping, as long as we shopped at the dollar store.

The fifty percent left over, or spending money, was theirs to spend however they wished. However, we did set some limits on how much they could spend on candy. (Now I look back and think maybe we should have required equal amounts for candy and the dentist.)

As a certified public accountant, part of me really liked this system because it prepared the children for the real world of money and paychecks. After you've paid all the tax withholding and set aside savings, you pretty much will have only about fifty percent of your pay left to live on anyway.

Since my children were accustomed to only being able to spend half of their allowance in the first place, you can imagine their frustration when they got a pay cut and no foreseeable prospect of a raise. Welcome to the real world, my dears.

When the complaining was complete, the children mutated into adaptable creatures who could turn just about anything around to their advantage. They discovered that even though they didn't have as much spending money as they used to, they did have a mother who, due to years of "working mom" guilt, could be easily convinced to do many, many things she never did for them when she worked full-time.

Suddenly, my "making" and "spreading" skills were in high demand. (Although with my Bookkeeper Bottom blossoming throughout my sedentary CPA years, I was already quite skilled in a different kind of spreading). They begged me to make their toast—"I can't spread the butter like you can, Mom;" their sandwiches—"I can't spread the peanut butter like you can, Mom;" and even their beds—"I can't spread the blankets out like you can, Mom".

This inability to spread conveniently occurred right at the time I became a stay-at-home mom. And I finally figured out that although we had cut into their allowances, they were "allowing" me to make it up to them in a lot of little ways.

When all was said and done, it had the makings of a good deal. My children had to give up money, but they gained a mom-servant who actually had time and energy to cook meals and even make cookies. Plus, I got to lick the bowls and knives (mental note to self: sharp side away from the tongue).

They also realized that yard work was seasonal, so the hard work with no pay was over before they knew it. It took me a little longer to realize that the time my children will spend actually at home and needing me is also for just a short while, so for now I'm trying to enjoy the "allowance" they give me a little bit more.

Bathtubs . . .

Big B, Little B,
What begins with B?
Bubbles in the bathtub,
Clean the bath and me.

For years and years, I didn't have time to take baths—let alone bubble baths. I had my shower down to two minutes and thirty seconds on hair-washing days and two minutes flat on days I didn't shampoo and condition. A shower was for cleaning my body, not relaxing. Ideas didn't flow to me as the water cascaded over my body in a rejuvenating stream. It was more like I made mental checklists of what I had to do that day as I lathered, rinsed, and did not repeat. I had things to do.

As for cleaning, I realized I would rather avoid using a bathtub than use it and have to clean it. I preferred to dust it, not scrub it. Soon it became necessary to have at least two bathtubs in my house—one for me to look at and dust semi-annually and one for my children to use. I didn't clean the children's tub; it was on their chore lists. I just pulled the shower curtain closed and when it got covered with mildew or pink cat ring (as Dr. Seuss might call it), I would simply buy a new one.

I was forced to reckon with the cleaning of the bathtub approximately once every three to seven years, which was how often we moved. I could even get out of it then if I was clever enough to assign my mother-in-law or helpful neighbor to clean that bathroom.

Sure, I felt the occasional twinge of guilt. When I caught a glimpse of the tub in the children's bathroom, I would shake my head, sigh, and murmur something like, "Those kids are such pigs; how can they stand such filth?" Then I would remember that pigs like to wallow in mud, and I would go dust my own bathtub.

For three years, I lived in a beautiful home with a master bathroom that was bigger than some people's first houses. It had a gorgeous, huge, jetted bathtub with sloping sides and steps leading up to it, and two big windows (with blinds) to allow sunlight to stream in. That bathroom, for me, was the selling point of the house. A person could have lived in that bathroom if only we'd installed a mini-fridge.

Unfortunately, having that bathroom meant cleaning that bathroom, so once again, the tub was only used occasionally so I wouldn't have to scrub it. The tub did have a nice quarry-tile area surrounding it, a perfect place for holding your book, Diet Coke, towel, telephone, and bath salts if you were so inclined to actually bathe in it. Did I mention it was fairly easy to dust?

When I decided to stop working outside the home, we put that majestic bathroom, and the attached house, up for sale. We were downsizing, and I could not expect such luxury in my next house. It was just as well, because luxury still has to be cleaned.

My husband and I looked at several houses that fit the required number of bedrooms and bathrooms. The houses in our budget range still claimed to have "master bathrooms," but they were more like "master wannabes." They still sported the separate "water closet" (toilet closed off from the rest of the room), but the double vanity, jetted tub, and two-man shower were not part of these "master" plans. In most cases, only a one-and-a-half man shower and no tub were part of the plan.

We almost settled for a house without a bathtub in the master bath, since we never really used the tub much anyway. Fortunately, we were saved from that mistake by revisiting a previously rejected house. When we had first seen it, the place smelled of pet odors, but when we came again, all the carpet had been replaced. The carpet was cheap, but it was no longer green, nor did it reek. Best of all, this house had a master bathroom with a shower and a bathtub. Not just a bathtub, but an almost-garden tub; and although you couldn't stretch out full-length in it, it had a comfortable sloping back, and you could prop your feet up against the shower wall if you wanted to fully submerge your torso and head.

I missed the fantasy tub in my old house and determined not to waste any more time dusting tubs because you just don't know when you might have to move into a house with no tub at all. There had to be a way to relax and use a tub, without wrenching your back scrubbing the thing. Too bad a maid was out of the question.

After quitting my job, one thing I had was time. I realized one morning, when the house was quiet, that I didn't have to take a two-minute shower. I could take a bubble bath!

Except I didn't have any bubble bath, not even cheap kids stuff. So I went to Bath and Body Works, who just happened to be having their semiannual 50–75 percent off sale. I stocked up on bath foam, and I'm not talking about the Mr. Bubble kind of detergent. I'm talking about aromatherapy bath products. I chose a lavender one for relaxing, a rose one for sensuality, and a juniper one for energy. If I mixed them up, I could be one sensually relaxed bundle of energy!

They smelled so good, I found myself using them every day. Addicted is a harsh word, but it was true—I started taking baths daily. I turned on the radio, opened a Diet Coke, and sank down into the relaxing, sensual, energetic water. Some days I spent five minutes, sometimes I spent fifteen minutes doing nothing but soaking in the tub. I gauged my bath time by how long it took to drink my Diet Coke—some days I gulped, some days I sipped. I even started shaving my legs more often than once a week. It seemed so wasteful to take a bubble bath every day, I felt guilty for this indulgence. I was actually relaxing every day—what a forbidden, forgotten pleasure!

I lay basking in the fragrant warmth, thankful that we had purchased a house with such a good tub, when it occurred to me that I would have to clean the tub now that I was using it so often. There is always a price to pay for paradise.

As I sipped my Diet Coke, I pondered my problem. My eye lit upon the scrunchy, netty thing that was gathering dust on the side of my bathtub. It had come with a gift set, one of those scrubbers that exfoliate while they slough off the dead skin. I had tried to use it a time or two, but I preferred a good, old-fashioned wash cloth. It sloughed off the dead skin in a gentler fashion.

That scrubby must be good for something, though. As I pulled the plug and the water started draining, I picked up the scrubby. I grabbed the soap and lathered up the thing and then tested it on the soap scum ring that was starting to form from my two straight weeks of bubble baths. Wow! The grey ring came right off with very little effort! I stood up in the tub so as not to get soap scum on me (except my legs, which I could easily wipe off since they were stubble-free now). I finished scrubbing the ring as the water drained. Then I rinsed the scrubby, picked up my used washcloth, and wiped down the edge of the tub where the shampoo bottle ring was forming and dust was settling. Now I was clean and the tub was clean. The scrubby had a purpose and I felt justified. I'm sure if the scrubby thing had feelings, it also would have felt justified.

I finished drying off and surveyed my tub as I got dressed. It was cleaner than I had ever seen it. I felt a sense of purpose too. I had indulged in my selfish bubble bath and cleaned the tub at the same time. Guilt erased, tub clean!

The only downside I can find to this situation is that Bath and Body Works doesn't have a 75 percent off sale more often. Oh, and my children's bathtub is still pretty gross—mostly because it's on their chore lists, not mine, and also because I don't touch pink cat ring.

Chores . . .

Big C, Little C,
Chores are hard to do,
They get a little easier,
When your kids pay you.

Getting children to do chores is kind of like herding cats—they run when they hear you coming, and it's easier just to ignore the whole issue. At some point though, you just have to empty the litter box—or their rooms—because the mess gets too nasty.

When you have three to six children (or any children, for that matter), there comes a time when you realize that if you don't teach them how to do chores and make them do the afore-mentioned chores, those children could be living off you and expecting you to clean up after them for the rest of your life. This suddenly begins to look very bleak, indeed.

I hardly had enough energy to do the bare minimum of chores at home when I was working full-time, let alone organize a wonderful method of teaching and implementing chores. I couldn't face tackling the enforcement of "daily jobs." I just didn't have the energy.

My husband and I finally agreed on the method we would employ: Saturday chores. This meant that every Saturday morning, first thing, we would print the chore lists off the computer. There were three to six different lists, dependent upon the number of children we had living at home at the time. In addition to the chore lists, they also had to clean their own rooms.

The lists would usually be separated according to rooms: kitchen, dining room, family room, upstairs bathroom, downstairs bathroom, and so on. These lists would rotate each week, so that each child would have the "opportunity" to clean different rooms. It was a fairly simple and straightforward method, and the lists usually looked something like this:

Family Room
- Gather and put away all belongings from room
- Dust furniture
- Vacuum floor
- Empty garbage

This list was usually interpreted as follows:
"MOM! He won't put away his stuff!"
"No! I'm using the vacuum now!"
"MOM! Whoever had this room last week did NOT empty the garbage!"

Then I would lecture the child(ren) on the fairness of the chore lists, threaten them throwing their stuff away if they didn't put it away immediately, and wrestle the vacuum cleaner hose away from the four-year-old before he sucked his eye out.

It seemed like it should have been so simple; at least, that's how Mary Poppins made it look. It wasn't simple, and it definitely wasn't fun—not for me, not for my husband, and definitely not for my children. I don't think my vacuum cleaner enjoyed it much, either. (Side note: Mary Poppins was not practically perfect; she was merely drawn that way).

We tried to stick with the chore lists, though. Even though it seemed like torture for us to teach our children how to work, we sustained ourselves with the belief that the efforts would someday be worth it.

We stood firm with the rule that there was no playing until the chores were done. Some of our children would rush through the chores at breakneck speed, doing a haphazard job of it. We countered that tactic by requiring them to bring us their list when it was finished, and then we would check off each item. Of course, we always found something they missed or had to re-do. However, I suspect they may have learned to leave some small, obvious thing undone, so that Mom or Dad could find something to make them do over, figuring that after that we would stop looking and they could go play.

Some of our other children procrastinated, completing their chores by whining, dawdling, eating, napping, or puttering until most of the Saturday was over and their friends had long since made other plans (or perhaps even advanced a grade in school). These same children sometimes greeted Sunday gratefully as a day of rest, thinking they had finally gotten out of their chores, only to be greeted on Monday by their unfinished chores and their wily little selves grounded.

Then there was the *one* child, the exception to the two

categories the others neatly fell into. This one child was a wheeler-dealer. He spent far more energy trying to weasel or deal his way out of chores than it ever would have taken him to actually do the chores himself.

For years, I couldn't figure out if this child was really, really smart or really, really lazy. Then I realized, one day, that he was actually both—he was smarzy. My smarzy child would bribe his siblings with things they couldn't resist—an electronic device for one, candy for another, if only they would do his chores.

Finally, we had to put our foot down and forbid him to make deals—until the other children begged us to let them make a deal with him. We tried to monitor the terms for fairness and hold the smarzy child accountable, but he kept on wheeling and dealing.

Eventually the other children grew wise to the deals and couldn't be bought as easily. This was about the time I quit work. Then the smarzy child turned his deal-making charms on me. He knew I had a soft spot for Ben & Jerry's Vanilla Caramel Fudge Ice cream (B&JVCF). When his brothers and sisters could no longer be bought, he discovered my price. When I wouldn't cave in for one pint of ice cream, he would offer two. He had a part-time job by this time and had money to spend; I had no money to spend, but lots of time—it was a win/win.

I had all of the ice cream I wanted, but I was then afflicted with the inability to eat less than a pint of Ben & Jerry's at a sitting. Whoever listed ½ cup as the serving size for that stuff was reality-impaired. It didn't take too long for my pants to notice the influx of pints, and my jeans rebelled by shrinking.

Faced with the very real possibility of only being able to wear XXXL pajama pants, I started saying no to the bribery. The smarzy child quickly searched for, and found, another angle. He had siblings who needed money, since their allowances had been cut or frozen, and he had money to pay for the chores that he hated to do.

I authorized the payment of money for chores. Thinking he had hit upon a sure-fire chore-avoidance scheme, the smarzy one advertised his willingness to pay to avoid hard labor. Unfortunately for him, my younger children had, by this time, learned to dislike additional chores more than they liked money. He appeared to be out of luck, until I realized that I suffered from lack of pocket change myself and had a need for Diet Coke money.

So I ended up doing my child's chores, and he paid me to do them. It didn't take me long because I didn't dawdle or spend my time trying to get out of them. I really don't have to wonder where he gets his smarziness from. (As a matter of fact, he started paying me to do his laundry next.) When I finished with his chores, I checked off my own list and let myself go outside to play afterwards, ice-cold Diet Coke in hand.

Dishes . . .

Big D, little D,
What begins with D?
The dishes in the dishwasher,
Don't look clean to me.

When I worked outside the home, the dishes always piled up at my house. Now that I don't work outside the home, the dishes still pile up at my house. I have always had the luxury of an automatic dishwasher, and in days past, my husband was very familiar with it. Now I am the one who spends time getting to know the dishwasher—rinsing the dishes, loading them, pressing the buttons to start the cycle, and then doing it all again the next day.

Because we tend to generate so many dirty dishes in one day (those kids expect to eat every day—usually several times a day!), doing the dishes is a never-ending job. I am not the first to discover that there is barely a nanosecond between the time you wash the last dish and another one turns up dirty. I'm also not the first to leave the clean dishes in the dishwasher until I'm ready to load the next batch of dirty ones.

This habit of leaving the clean dishes in until I was ready

to do the next load resulted in my kids often going to the cupboard that should contain glasses, opening it, finding it empty, going to the dishwasher, opening it, and yelling, "Are the dishes in the dishwasher clean?"

This happened at least once a day, and they couldn't seem to grasp the fact that I didn't leave dirty dishes in the dishwasher—my loading it always resulted in a full load, and I always ran it when it was full.

To me, the obvious answer was: "If the dishwasher is full of dishes, they are clean." Even if my children couldn't figure out my pattern of storing the clean dishes in the dishwasher, I figured they could open the dishwasher and:

1) see no food on the dishes, and,
2) smell no nasty smell from dirty dishes.

Apparently it was easier for them to yell the question rather than just look with their own eyes.

I could have changed my habit and unloaded the dishwasher when it was finished, thereby using my cupboards for actually storing the clean dishes, but the energy expenditure of putting away dishes would be greater than that of yelling, "Yes, they're clean!" So instead, I just kept complaining about my children's inability to discern dirty dishes from clean ones.

I was muttering to my husband one night about how the kids had never learned that the dishes in the dishwasher were clean, and he pointed out that it was kind of hard to tell if they were clean or dirty. With his remark, it occurred to me that I may have discovered a genetic source for my children's denseness, but then he continued.

"We all rinse our dishes when we clear our places. Then you rinse them again as you load the dishwasher. There really isn't a good way to tell if the dishes are clean or dirty. We also have hard water, so the glasses look like they're dirty when they're clean." He thought he was being helpful, but he wasn't.

"I can tell they're clean. I just don't see how it's so hard to figure out if a dishwasher full of dishes is clean or dirty." Fortunately for him, he didn't suggest I actually put them away after they were clean—he had learned something in the twenty-plus years we had been married.

Because I like to prove my point until everyone around agrees with me (my husband refers to it as "beating a dead horse"), I mulled around in my brain for a way to teach my family a lesson about clean dishes.

We went out for pizza a few nights later and, as we were stuffing our faces, I casually mentioned, "I found a way to cut expenses by a few more dollars a month." It got my husband's attention, and I knew my children were listening as well.

"I thought about what you said about us rinsing the dishes so much that you can't really tell if the dishes in the dishwasher are dirty or clean. Since no one can tell if they're dirty or clean, I rinsed the dishes, loaded the dishwasher, and, instead of running it, I just left them there. I wondered if anyone would notice. So far, no one has. I figure we can save about four dollars a month on detergent and at least that much on the utility bills, since we're not heating as much water by actually running the dishwasher."

My husband just looked at me and kept eating. He knew

what I was doing. The four children who were with us sat there with gaping jaws and pizza slices frozen midway to their mouths, hoping they had heard me wrong. Finally one said, "You're kidding, right?"

I smiled and said, "It's not like any of you could tell the difference. You know we're trying to save money."

"But you really are washing them, aren't you?" the one persisted—the others just looked sick. I briefly contemplated eating their share of the remaining pizza but took pity on them after seeing their nauseated looks.

"Of course I wash them," I relented. I couldn't resist adding, "But you guys really wouldn't know if I did or didn't."

I proved my point. Whatever that point was. They recovered enough to polish off the pizza that night, and they still ask me, "Are the dishes in the dishwasher clean?" I still answer, "Yes!" But they do peer at the dishes a little more skeptically now before they use them. All of them but one—he won't use any of our cups or glasses now, except for a special plastic one that he holds toward the light to exam for residue. He may even sniff it before use. That's fewer glasses for me to load in the dishwasher, so it's all good.

Exercise . . .

Big E, Little E,
E . . . E . . . E
Exercise is for everyone,
Even you and me.

We live in a world driven by convenience. We drive up to the bank and to fast food. We park as close as we can to the doors of stores or, better yet, we cybershop from the comfort of our desks at work or armchairs at home. We watch TV with remotes in hand as we text our friends on our cell phones.

My favorite chair is a recliner with a cooler in one arm and a phone in the other. It has massage and heat built right in. My laptop computer rests in a holder on one side, with my crocheting and a big bookshelf on the other side. If my chair had a Porta Potty in it, and the Diet Coke delivery man would come up a few stairs, I would never have to get up.

I've read reports of people getting so obese that they can't stand up or walk anymore. I realize that in my chair, I could pretty much survive if people would keep tossing me truffles and popcorn. I also am aware that if I don't get up and move, I could easily outgrow my chair.

I have always been one of those Americans whose BMI (body mass index) is at the upper limit of acceptable. For years I blamed it on "Bookkeeper Bottom" or "CPA Spread." When I hit the lovely milestone of forty, I realized the acreage would just keep on spreading like suburban sprawl.

I have tried all of the usual things over the years. I have dieted and exercised, although rarely in sync. I've tried pills and powders and twenty-minute workouts. Sometimes I'm successful, but mostly it's been an ongoing battle of the bulge.

My children have witnessed my dedication, or lack thereof, to losing weight. They've made fun of me as I work out to exercise videos, calling the others to come and watch or making a game out of it. They would toss a ball at me as I kicked to Tae-bo or Denise Austin and giggle as my foot made contact, sending the ball soaring.

When they were really young and not so mocking, they would join me when I worked out. They would put on their own "work-out clothes" and move along beside me, dodging the bullets of sweat that shot from me in every direction.

As they got older, when they weren't making fun of me, they would sometimes encourage me in their own sadistic way. One night I got on the treadmill as we watched a Utah Jazz basketball game on TV. There wasn't much time left in the game, maybe forty-five seconds, but I knew it could easily drag into fifteen or twenty minutes, so I convinced myself to get in a little workout.

I announced that I was going to work out until the game was over. When my treadmill hit the fifteen minute mark, the game went into overtime. Another five minutes on the game clock—translating to at least fifteen more on the treadmill. I voiced out loud that I didn't plan on overtime, and my son conveniently pointed out that I had said I would workout until the game was over and it wasn't over. I stubbornly kept going.

At the thirty minute mark, the game went into double overtime. My flaccid legs were like Jell-O, and I was ready to quit—again. My son once more reminded me of my words and convinced me to keep going, so I did.

Forty-five minutes later, when I was sweat-soaked and panting, the Jazz won and I was able to stop. My son smirked at my fatigue and his success at pressuring me to "go the extra mile (or four)." I was proud of my workout, and it probably would have helped even more if weeks or months didn't pass before my next outburst of exercise.

In the past year or two, I have been able to establish an aerobic exercise routine. The wonderful equipment I accumulated over the years has actually been put to work as more than clothes horses. I stay off the treadmill during NBA games, though, as I don't want to get too physically fit. Now, if I can just work on eating right.

My husband is still trying to implement a workout schedule for himself. When we down-sized into our current home, we lost the luxury of an exercise room. His weight machine and free weights found a home in the garage, which is not conducive to working out, especially in the winter months when it's cold enough to store meat in there.

My husband was excited when our son moved away to college and vacated his bedroom. I was just excited that he moved away. When the oldest two left for college, we had an agreement with them to keep their bedrooms intact for a year. That was back in the day when we had more room and a bigger house. When we moved, we left some of our compassion in the old house, as well.

We explained to our son that we would not be able to keep his room exclusively for him for the first year of college, which caused some grumbling from him. I carefully, and just a little gleefully, packed up the belongings he left behind and stored them in the closet. We did leave a bed set up in the room so he would have a place to sleep when he came home to visit.

My husband went to work disassembling the weight machine in the garage in anticipation of once again having an exercise room. But in his zeal to relocate the equipment, he dropped a seventy-pound piece of the weight machine on his big toe, nearly severing it, and breaking it in several places—the toe, not the weight machine.

When the toe healed and the weight machine, benches, and weights were moved into my son's vacated room, my husband commenced his workout plan, complete with clipboard and progress charts.

His enthusiasm was dampened by only two events—life and the fact that my son came home from college every weekend. Life got in the way of his weekday workouts because his days were already filled with more than he had time to do. My son coming home on weekends got in the way because he reinhabited his room, strewing stuff about, sleeping until noon, and complaining about how we took over his room as soon as he moved out (I didn't have the heart to tell him about the jig I danced as I packed his belongings).

Needless to say, we are not the best examples to our children of how to exercise. But we have managed to sneak a little exercise into their lives without calling it such.

When our children exhibit bad manners at the table, my husband is appalled. He cannot stand to hear them belch loudly at the dinner table (a talent I taught them, courtesy of my love for carbonated beverages). He already knows that I am semi-responsible for teaching them the art of burping, but I know when to refrain from doing it, and my children haven't mastered that part of the talent yet.

So he implemented the consequence of pushups for belching infractions. If a child accidentally (or on purpose) let one rip at the dinner table, that child had to do ten pushups.

The solution worked remarkably well. It was even effective enough that we used it for other undesirable behavior, such as leaving their dirty socks in the middle of the living room floor or general unchecked rowdiness.

Our children developed strong arms from this method of discipline. When it came time for physical fitness testing at school, they were average in sit-ups and pull-ups, but always excelled in doing push-ups.

We didn't limit it to just our own children. Once, when we were traveling home from visiting some relatives, we had two of the cousins with us. The kids were all being loud and rowdy and had been warned to settle down. After a couple of warnings, my husband threatened to pull over and make them do push-ups.

I guess they didn't believe he would really make them do push-ups alongside the freeway, but that is just what he did.

He pulled off to the side, almost in the ditch. He ordered them out, down the embankment, and had them all do push-ups; except for the one cousin who was not misbehaving.

They were all quiet the rest of the way home and still talk about the embarrassment of having their dad pull over to make them do push-ups along the freeway.

As they get older and we get older, they are quick to point out behavior that my husband and I do that qualifies for push-ups. I've noticed it's mainly me—my husband doesn't belch at the table. But I'm happy to say that I can do fifty push-ups now (and not the girly ones either). I have a goal of being able to do one hundred. Maybe I'll have another Diet Coke and get started.

Food . . .

Big F, Little F,
What gives me a fright?
A cookie monster tossing up,
Her cookies through the night.

In our household, we have a fine appreciation for the sweeter things in life—namely most foods that are sweet. If it has sugar and chocolate, it meets my nutritional requirements. I have a little decorative plaque hanging in my kitchen that states, "This kitchen serves the four basic food groups: chocolate fudge, chocolate brownies, chocolate ice cream, and diet cola."

This mantra has served me well over the years. Even at my lowest energy levels, I managed to whip up homemade chocolate chip cookies or hot fudge brownies on a regular basis. I'm not much of a chef when it comes to creating meals, but desserts are a different story.

My family pays me the high honor of saying my homemade chocolate chip cookies are the best they've ever tasted. Whether this is actually so, their flattery has had the desired results—I keep making cookies.

Those coveted chocolate chip cookies are not all sugar and spice and everything nice; they have been the source of some decisions in my life that I'm not too proud of. I blame the cookies, but I really should bear the brunt of the blame.

You see, whenever I make a batch of those cookies, my children clamor for as many as they can stuff into their faces. Apparently, they get that talent from me since their father has self-control in that area.

Even as a child, I loved to make cookies. I would cry to my mom when my brothers and sisters would gobble them up as fast as they came out of the oven. My mom assured me that the rate at which they were consumed was proof positive that my cookies were delicious. In my opinion, my siblings didn't even chew them, much less actually taste them. In spite of my inability to control their consumption, I kept making cookies.

When my own children tried to swoop down on the fresh cookies, I always limited them to three or four cookies each. I wanted the treats to last a couple of days at least, and I was concerned that they would make themselves sick. They always begged for more, but like any good mother (and cookie miser), I set the limits they couldn't set for themselves.

One evening I got tired of the whining. My oldest daughter was about seven at the time and had been pestering me for more and more cookies. Finally, I decided this was a lesson she needed to learn for herself. I told her, "You can have as many cookies as you want." She searched my face, suspecting trickery, but when she confirmed my permission with a "Really?" and I nodded—that was all she needed.

That evening she ate as many cookies as she wanted. I can't remember how many she ate, but I would guess it was around ten or twelve. She complained afterwards that her tummy hurt but got very little sympathy from me. At bedtime, I shooed her off to bed and she dutifully climbed in, in spite of her stuffed stomach.

An hour or two later, she woke up crying. She called out to me, and I went to her room just in time to see her sitting up in bed, throwing up—literally "tossing her cookies."

I cleaned her up, changed the bedding, and comforted her so she could go back to sleep. I pondered later about whether or not she had learned a lesson. I think I was the one who learned the greater lesson—not only did I feel bad that I had allowed my daughter to make herself sick by overeating cookies, I also had to clean up the mess.

When I recalled that episode, it brought to mind another cookie incident that had occurred a couple of years earlier. We had just moved back to Utah from California and were staying in my sister-in-law's basement. We were struggling financially; they weren't much better off, and we were trying to save up money to get into our own place again.

I went to the kitchen to make cookies, which was a rare treat at that time. I had set the margarine out to soften and when I returned I found that my two-year-old nephew had discovered the joys of smearing an entire cube of margarine all over his naked-except-for-his-diaper body.

We cleaned up the mess, got out another stick of margarine, and I proceeded to make the cookie dough. That was when my sister-in-law set her four-month-old baby on the counter to give him his medicine for reflux. Just at that moment, he "refluxed," as he was prone to do. Sadly, I didn't move the cookie dough out of the way in time.

The precious cookie dough had been sprayed with baby formula, right from the baby's mouth. Most people would have thrown the dough out, but those ingredients were not cheap, and our appetite for cookies had been whetted.

We had to make a judgment call. The entire bowl of dough was not affected, just part of it. We decided to scrape out the contaminated portion, rather than "toss our cookies" completely. We salvaged what was left, baked the cookies, and thoroughly enjoyed them.

I look back at the cookie incidents and realize that as parents, we often find ourselves in situations like the cookie episodes. When you give in to the whining, in spite of your better judgment, often you are left to clean up the mess.

Sometimes you clean up one mess, only to have another one created almost immediately. You have to make judgments based on what you have to work with, and life is usually less than ideal. Even when it looks like you may have to throw out the whole batch, some parts are usually salvageable.

My children still try to eat as many cookies as I let them, and I still limit their intake. Now my oldest daughter makes cookies for her family, and although she restricts how many her own daughters can eat, she lets her two youngest siblings eat as many as they want. Could that be her way of getting even?

Since my granddaughter has reflux, I am careful to keep the cookie dough out of her shooting range. I still believe chocolate is its own food group and will cure most of what ails you, if the quantities imbibed in one sitting are not too large. It's also not too shabby when it's been sprayed with baby formula.

Garbage . . .

A B C D E F G,
Garbage gets to go outside,
G . . . G . . . G

It seems like the more children you have, the more garbage you generate. Not all of it winds up in the garbage can; it seems like I find a great deal of it in their rooms, on the floor.

For some unfathomable reason, it seems to be easier to drop a candy wrapper on the floor and walk over it or kick it several times, rather than throw it in the garbage can that is three feet away when the candy is first unwrapped.

When you point out the trash on the floor, the child looks in the direction of your finger and asks in a pseudo-innocent voice, "What?" It's almost as if there is a force field around the garbage that makes it invisible to those under the age of twenty. Maybe they just expect us to believe it is invisible to them.

An interesting phenomenon occurs when trash actually does make it into the garbage can. The garbage can be filled to overflowing, but apparently children are unable to see the garbage that is actually in the can as well. They simply put one more thing on top. It's like a game. If it stays in the can, they've scored; if it tumbles out, it's someone else's turn to play, and they move on.

The game of garbage has rules that a parent can't be privy to, let alone understand. For example: Why does a milk carton stay in the fridge with only ten drops of milk left in it, yet the plastic ring that once sealed the milk jug gets left on the countertop? Why does the graham cracker box sit on the pantry shelf, empty, as if it's about to refill itself? Why does that delicious casserole you made for dinner end up in the garbage, not just on top, but buried deep beneath the empty cereal boxes you pulled out from between your son's bed and the wall?

These are all part of the garbage game; pieces of one of the many unsolved mysteries of parenthood. I cannot join the game under their rules, so I invented a couple of my own.

Since it is a game, I allow them each to be a winner at some point. When the kitchen garbage is overflowing (which occurs at least once a day, in spite of all the trash left on the floors of their rooms), I look for the child closest at hand.

I then call out their name and enthusiastically say "You're a winner, winner, winner!" I pull out the bag of garbage and hand it to them. I then tell them that I will replace the garbage bag while they run their "prize" out to the trash can.

It's a little hard for them to deny the task—after all they've just been called a winner. Everyone likes to be a winner. If by chance they *do* whine, I offer a compromise; they get to take out the garbage *and* replace the bag.

With my system, they get to be a winner and do only half the chore. Of course, they tend to scurry away when they see me heading to the garbage can and pulling out the full bag.

The other part of the garbage game that I've added is the part that involves me nagging them to clean up their rooms. About half of my children will clean their rooms after only a nag or two. The remainder will do just about anything—even homework or bathing—to avoid cleaning their rooms.

These children have forced me to implement the "Mom will clean your room for you" option. It isn't an option they want, but several have chosen it by default.

When I clean their rooms, I take in two big garbage bags. One is for all of the garbage, and the other is for their belongings, which will have to be earned back. A real downside to Mom cleaning your room is that many, many things that look like garbage to Mom are not garbage to a child. Darn!

Another downside is that the items Mom has deemed not to be garbage must be earned back, one at a time, by doing extra chores. There are times when it takes more than two bags, and times when unclaimed, unearned property becomes garbage due to inaction on the part of the cleanee. After all, the garage shelves can only hold so many bags.

I have a couple of sons who have had their rooms cleaned by me more than once. They pretend not to care, although they are quick to hover and snatch, trying to rescue a precious He-Man action figure or Air Soft gun from the garbage game.

There are lessons that take a while for some of us to learn. For instance, I could have become a yard-sale queen and made my millions (okay, maybe hundreds) by selling the bits of junk and treasures I stuffed into garbage bags during my cleaning frenzies. Alas, I've always been more of a woman on the edge than an entrepreneur.

I may look like a mean mommy when I haul out those bags of garbage from their rooms, but I confess that for a brief moment in time, I feel like a "winner, winner, winner!" And we all like to be winners.

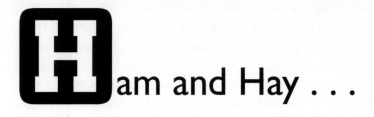

Ham and Hay . . .

Big H, Little H,
Hungry for some ham?
How does hay grow that way?
Helpful is what I am.

Perhaps you've noticed that as a parent you sometimes color things to make them more palatable to your child—or maybe you do it just to mess with your child's mind. I have been guilty of both and have always considered it fair payback for the mental anguish my children have inflicted on me.

One of my sons hated peanut butter from the time he was tiny. We quickly found out why when he was diagnosed with a peanut allergy that caused serious allergic reactions. This child needed an alternative to peanut butter sandwiches (which were a staple in my house). He zeroed in on "ham and jam" sandwiches.

The sandwiches were actually made of bologna and jelly because we couldn't afford real ham. But we called bologna "ham" and my children didn't know the difference. It also provided a much catchier name—"ham and jam" sounds much more appetizing than "bologna and jelly." It was several years before my children realized that real ham existed and tasted a lot better than bologna, especially when they learned that jam wasn't a particularly great condiment for meat sandwiches of any sort.

I taught my children that graham crackers were "cookies," which I figured was a pretty harmless and fairly common exaggeration. Not as much sugar, not as expensive. It worked for me. However, I didn't stop there at twisting their little minds.

We kept a food storage supply, and one thing we had a stock of was powdered milk. Now, I have never liked powdered milk and did not drink it or give it to my children on a regular basis. It was in my food storage for emergencies. I didn't like to think about what kind of emergency it would take to induce me to actually drink powdered milk, but I kept it on hand, just in case.

When we ran out of milk one morning, I deemed it an "emergency" and mixed up some of the powdered milk for the kids to use on their cereal. I had to do it surreptitiously, knowing that if my children even suspected I was trying to feed them powdered milk, they would refuse to try it. I was successful in my sneakiness, poured their cereal and milk, and set it before them.

My daughter took a couple of bites and announced, "This milk tastes funny." I had been caught, which wasn't too surprising, considering the taste is a little hard to disguise. I tried to recover the situation with a little humor.

"That's because it's cat's milk," I said with a straight face, continuing about my business. The spoon dropped, and she shrieked in horror. I tried to recover the situation with the truth—after all, how bad could powdered milk be, when you compared it to cat's milk?

"It isn't cat's milk, honey. I was teasing. It's really powdered milk. We ran out of regular milk so I mixed up powdered milk for the cereal. That's why it tastes different." My stratagem did not work. She refused to eat the cereal and was very suspicious of milk thereafter.

In my defense, some of these spins are to make a less-than-desirable offering look or sound enticing. But sometimes I do it just to mess with them.

One day we were driving down the road and we passed a farmer's field that was covered with freshly baled hay. The bales were at perfect intervals and I commented on them.

My daughter said, "That's a lot of hay." I agreed and went on to tease her.

"It is a lot of hay. I am just amazed that they can get it to grow in bales like that."

She took the bait and looked at the bales of hay with renewed interest. "Really? It grows like that? I thought they did it with a machine." She was amazed.

"No, it grows like that. It's just unbelievable." I kept a straight face, but my son in the back seat started snickering, and my daughter figured out I was teasing her—again.

"You're so rude!"

I hear that comment a lot.

She still reminds me of the time I tricked her into believing in leprechauns. She was about nine years old, and on St. Patrick's Day, her babysitter put little footprints all over her house and told the kids that they were leprechaun footprints. They followed the footprints and found a little treat—some licorice—at the end of the trail.

My daughter was excited and told me all about it. She wondered why the leprechaun never came to our house. I suggested she might try writing him a letter. I stopped by her room a little while later and saw a note folded on her bed, addressed to the leprechaun, with a piece of licorice enclosed. She wasn't around, so I read it.

The note asked him to come to our house and make some things green, asked him what things he liked, and if she could meet him. It was so cute, I decided she needed to hear back, personally, from the leprechaun. I took the letter and licorice with me.

The next day I bought some green gum and green notebooks, and answered her letter in cleverly disguised handwriting. I explained that I (the leprechaun) couldn't turn things green, because her parents might not like it, but that I was leaving some green things for her and her brothers. I (the leprechaun) told her I liked a lot of green things, especially money and broccoli (a nice touch—go, Mom!). I also let her know that she couldn't meet me, because then I would have to lead her to my pot of gold.

I left the note, gum, and notebooks on her bed, slightly under her covers. She came home and found them. She was astounded, not suspecting me at all, since she had not told me about the note and licorice. I shared in her astonishment, read the note with her, and enjoyed the magic of the moment.

The next day, she came home from school angry at some

of her friends. She had told them about the leprechaun, and they all insisted that there was no such thing as leprechauns. She stood up for herself and told them she had proof! She was so mad at them for doubting her that I had to come clean.

I told her what I did, and she didn't believe me at first. She offered up the evidence that clearly the handwriting was not mine. I showed her how I did it. She asked me about her note and the licorice, and I admitted I took them. She was furious at me. I offered to return the piece of licorice. She accused me of lying to her and demanded to know what else I had lied about. I asked her if she really wanted to know.

After exposing Santa Claus and the Easter Bunny, she was even angrier at me. She asked why parents would lie to their children, and I tried to explain to her about the fun and magic of believing in those kinds of things. She felt like she had made a fool of herself in front of her friends. I told her to blame me and that it wasn't her fault.

She eventually forgave me, but still gets a little thunderous when leprechauns are mentioned. I don't think she can eat Lucky Charms to this day.

At the time, it made me think that maybe I tease my children too much. But the remorse didn't last, and when my children mention that the milk tastes funny, I still tell them it's cat's milk. Maybe someday they will figure out what the expiration date on the carton means. Then again, they may just decide to get even with me—which is why I never drink milk.

Ice Cream . . .

Big I, Little I,
What begins with I?
Ice cream is appealing,
'Til it ends up on your thighs.

I have a theory that God created teenagers to prepare us for the time our children need to leave the nest. If we had to say goodbye to our cuddly little babies, precocious chubby toddlers, or gap-toothed first graders, our hearts would break.

Teenagers do something to that soft-heartedness. By the time they have shared their stubborn, you-were-never-like-me attitude with us for several years, most parents are packing the suitcases for their offspring, holding the door open, and sometimes even offering money—if they'll JUST GO!

Every child is unique, and each one possesses an uncanny ability to push his parents' buttons. They reveal some of those buttons to their siblings but hold some back for their own personal use against us, the parents.

One button-pushing afternoon, after my teenage daughter and I had been on each other's nerves all day long, we went to the grocery store together. We were both kind of muttering under our breath, grumbling about something.

As we walked down the produce aisle, a little girl who was two or three sat in her cart calling out, "Hey, you!" We were caught up in our own sour moods, and paid little attention to the toddler. "Hey, you!" she called again.

My daughter walked past the cart and a chubby little hand snaked out, grabbing her arm. "Look at me!" the little girl demanded of my teenager. My daughter stopped and looked at the girl. Seeing she had my daughter's full attention, she continued. "Say 'ice cream,'" she urged my daughter.

My daughter sort of smiled and repeated to the girl, "Ice cream," after which the little girl beamed, patted my daughter's arm and said encouragingly, "Good!"

We both laughed at the little girl, and the interchange lightened our moods considerably. When we got home, we shared the story with the rest of the family and laughed again. The contention and sour moods had disappeared.

That happened many years ago, but even now I can email or text my husband or daughter with "Hey, you! Look at me. Say 'ice cream!'" and I know it is guaranteed to make them break out in smiles.

It is true that ice cream, in and of itself, is enough to make most people smile. Ice cream seems to have either a celebratory connection or a therapeutic application. We use it both ways in my family. It's your birthday? Let's have ice cream with our cake! Win first place in the science fair? Let's go get ice cream! Got your first publishing contract? Here we come, Cold Stone Creamery! Had a root canal? Sip on this milk shake! Feeling depressed and lonely? Bring on the Ben & Jerry's Vanilla Caramel Fudge!

Maybe this love of ice cream is instilled in us when we are tiny. When the ice cream truck cruises through the neighborhood on a stifling-hot summer day playing loud, off-key music over and over, like a freaky jack-in-the-box run amok, kids scurry off to their parents begging for ice cream money. Parents give in to make the begging stop (and also to get "Pop Goes the Weasel" to pop down another street). As kids, we weren't concerned so much with quality as we were with quantity. This seemed to change as we grew older—which brings me back to the Ben & Jerry's ice cream.

I wasn't aware of the existence of Ben & Jerry's until one summer when I sent my three oldest children on an airplane trip to Vermont to visit their grandma. She took them to see many sights, including Lenny the Chocolate Moose, but they all three agreed that the tour of Ben & Jerry's ice cream factory was a high point. I couldn't imagine how ice cream could be that extraordinary until I purchased some and introduced it to my thighs, via my mouth and stomach. My palate hasn't been satisfied with ordinary ice cream since.

My children getting me hooked on premium ice cream had some interesting side benefits for all. It was expensive—"premium" in price as well as taste—so I needed some major inducement, besides my appetite, to purchase it. Soon it became a sought-after commodity in my household, all the more desirable for its rarity.

I found that when I could no longer pay money to an older child to watch the younger children, I could entice that same child to tend with promise of payment in the form of a pint of Ben & Jerry's—choice of flavor to be determined. Even at the premium price, it was still a good deal when you considered the going rate for babysitters.

It seemed like a pretty good arrangement and lasted for quite awhile. Then, as my teenagers blossomed into that metamorphosis stage that contains the promise of eventually becoming human again, they discovered they could convince me to do things by offering to pick up a pint of Ben & Jerry's for me—sometimes even offering to pay for it themselves, if the stakes were high enough.

They also learned to walk through the freezer section of whatever grocery store we happened to be in to see if Ben & Jerry's was on sale—they knew I couldn't resist a bargain. They would hurry back to inform me of the sale price and that my favorite flavor beckoned. I had to fight two temptations: 1) the creamy satisfaction of sugar, cream, and caramel in a convenient 1,160 calorie portion (I can't eat just half a pint); and 2) the opportunity of saving money.

So, I taught my children well. Too well, I discovered, as I struggled to get my pants on over my ice-cream-craving, sale-loving thighs. I had to learn to practice saying "ice cream" rather than eating it all the time. And now my husband points out that I'm saving even more money by not buying it at all.

Saying "ice cream" still feels good and makes me smile, and the aftermath isn't as hard on my jeans or my wallet.

Jaguar . . .

Big J, Little J.
How does it begin?
Jaguar XJR always can
Evoke a grin.

There are two words that are guaranteed to make my husband smile. Anyone can walk by him and whisper these words, and they will always get a grin. The two words are "jaguar" and "supercharged."

In our household, it was always the rule that I got to drive the nicest vehicle, just as it should be. When my husband had a 1988 Chevy Corvette, I drove a 2001 Chevy Tahoe. He loved the Corvette (a.k.a. The Money Pit), but it wouldn't evoke a smile like the word "jaguar" did.

He has always wanted to own a Jaguar XJ series. In 2003, he finally got a black 1986 Jaguar Vanden Plas. It was a classy-looking car, and we picked it up for about $3,800. At the time, I drove a 2003 Chevy Suburban LT, for which we paid about $38,000. That's right—ten times more than the Jaguar.

But he drove that black Jag and loved it, especially after having to sell the Corvette. He kept it washed and polished, and it looked good. We moved into a new neighborhood a few months after he got it as part of our downsizing when I quit working full time.

I was happy with my charcoal Suburban with power everything—especially the leather heated seats. But invariably, when we met any of our new neighbors, the male half of the couple would say something to my husband like, "Oh you drive the Jaguar," in a tone of reverential awe.

I wanted to yell, "My Suburban cost ten times more than that old black hunk of junk!" but I didn't, for two reasons: one, I figured out that owning a Jaguar was a dream that many men harbored; and two, the black 1986 Jaguar Vanden Plas already did not like me.

It ran well for my husband, but when I drove it, something would always go wrong. It died more than once on a busy street. Perhaps it sensed I thought much more of my Suburban than I did of that car, or maybe old cars just break down more often. Whatever the reason, I avoided driving it.

We ended up selling my Suburban to pay off bills and save money. It was hard for me to see it go, but I liked living indoors and eating more than I liked driving the Suburban.

I needed a car to drive, so we bought a 1999 Chevrolet Lumina from my husband's grandmother, who passed away shortly after we purchased it—I don't think the two things were related. The car had low miles on it, got good gas mileage, and was dependable. And did I mention cheap?

The black Jaguar sucked our wallets dry. It was almost as bad as the white Corvette had been. When something broke on it, you could estimate what the part would reasonably cost.

Then you needed to double that and add a couple hundred dollars. My handy husband could do many repairs himself, but the black Jag still became a black hole.

We discussed the possibility of ceasing to pour money into it and getting a newer car. And when I suggested to my husband that it was time, he had a list of newer Jaguars to go look at the very next day.

I confess, I cringed at the thought. I wanted a reliable vehicle, which contradicted my opinion of Jaguars. I sure liked the way he smiled when I said "jaguar" though, so I agreed to look at the cars.

We went to drive a couple of 2001 Jaguar XJRs. The first one was hammered, but the second one—a silver, elegant thing—looked and drove like a dream. After I drove it, I was hooked, and I agreed to the purchase. Now, I'm smart enough to know that XJ was still the body style my husband liked the best. But I wasn't smart enough to know what the "R" in XJR stood for, and I didn't ask until after we bought it.

Trying in vain to keep a straight face, he told me it stood for "supercharged." We had just purchased a car that was as fast as the Corvette he once owned but drove so smoothly I thought it was a luxury sedan. He was fighting a smile of triumph, so I whispered "supercharged" to see what would happen. His face nearly ripped in half from the power of his smile. He was one happy guy.

It takes me a while to figure some things out, but I finally did. Somehow things got mighty twisted. I was driving my husband's dead grandmother's car, the "Luminator," and he was driving a "supercharged" Jaguar XJR that originally cost more than our first house. Of course, we were far too cheap to pay that much for it, but that was beside the point.

The Luminator started to slowly fall to pieces. The cup holder broke, the weather stripping on the door hung off, and, thanks to one of my children, the driver's side mirror broke into pieces when it met the side of the garage as the car was being backed out. I told my husband about each thing breaking, but it seems his mind would go blank once he got into his supercharged Jaguar.

I used crazy glue to put the casing of the mirror back on, and I even felt a strange affinity to it, seeing as how we were both cracked. But when I came out to find the pieces of the mirror on the garage floor again, I began to murmur. I started hearing strange whistling noises as I drove the Luminator, and it wasn't me. I was sure it would break down at any moment.

One day, after stopping at a neighbor's house, I grabbed the gear-shift lever to put it in drive, and the entire lever came off in my hand. I sat there holding the lever, trying to process what to do. The only possibility I could come up with was to keep driving and never stop, considering the means to shift the transmission was detached from the car—I was locked in eternal drive.

Realizing that option wouldn't work, I kept one foot on the brake while I blindly pawed around for the clip that had come out of the base of the lever, where it attached to the steering wheel column. I found the clip, held the lever in place, and frantically tried to lodge it back in its little slot, while trying not to run over the neighbor's mail box.

I got the lever reattached and was able to shift into park

when I pulled into the garage. Parking never felt so good. But even that episode didn't spur my husband to action.

The final straw came when my husband complained that his cup holder latch on the Jaguar was broken, and he needed to order a new part—to the tune of about $120. It was the latch, not the cup holder—it could still hold a beverage. If he even used his cup holder. I ranted because I actually *did* use mine—a lot—until it literally broke off (kind of like the gearshift lever, only I couldn't get it back together), and I'd suffered cold thighs ever since from holding my soda between my legs as I drove.

My raving stopped him from ordering the cup holder for his car, but it didn't induce him to fix mine. It wasn't until I told him the Luminator was making a strange noise and actually asked him to drive it for a few days that change finally came. (Mental note to self: he always says hints don't work and I just need to come out and ask for what I want. Maybe he thought I was just venting all that time. Maybe he really means hints don't work.)

It took one day of my husband driving the Luminator to get a new mirror put on. He inserted the clip on the steering wheel column all the way—apparently I didn't fix it completely. He even offered to replace the cup holder, but by then I'd graduated to one-liter bottles of water that wouldn't fit in the cup holder anyway, so I declined. (Mental note to self: give him a cup holder for his birthday for the Jaguar. Oh wait, I already did that for Father's Day.)

So I still drive my husband's dead grandmother's car, and he still drives a supercharged Jaguar XJR. If you meet him sometime, just say either word ("jaguar" or "supercharged") and watch him split a grin.

I said things got twisted, and I always used to get the best car in the household. I left out one part of the deal. The next car we get will be mine. A Silver Ice Metallic 2010 Chevy Camaro SS. They just became available as I write this, and when I've saved up my pennies, dollars, and pots of gold, the Luminator will go into retirement and then you can whisper "supercharged" to my husband and "supersport" to me and we'll all be smiling. Except for my children, who are still fighting over who gets the cars when we die.

Karate . . .

Big K, little K,
What begins with K?
Karate kicks by your kids,
Make teachers go quite gray.

Several years ago, we enrolled our two oldest children in karate. I watched them for a few months and secretly harbored a desire to join them in their classes. Apparently, punishing myself mentally isn't enough; I need occasional physical humiliation as well.

My third child was five when he decided he wanted to start taking lessons too. My sister-in-law and her five-year-old agreed to join us, and thus the karate years began.

We went faithfully. My sister-in-law and I were the two oldest in the class and, in all likelihood, the most comical. She actually had talent, and I tried to keep up with her. Our sensei was a man about our age who seemed to take delight in baiting us. After he paired up the children to spar with one another, he would spar with his two adult students individually. Just as I was feeling pretty good about my blocks and attempts to jab at him, he would block hard with his arm (leaving a big bruise on my forearm) and follow through with a nice slap on the head, letting me know he could have easily knocked me out cold. I think my ego was bruised even more than my arm.

My five-year-old and his cousin were a sight to behold. In their tiny gis, they would kick their legs straight out and throw punches that were several inches short of contact, yelling "Aye Aye Aye" (ki ai-ing).

I vowed to stay a white belt forever in order to avoid the humiliation of standing with rows of four-foot-high ninja-wannabes, trying to master basic forms one and two in an attempt to increase rank. Earning the next belt color, or even tape on my belt, designating that I was "high" in my color rather than "low," seemed completely overrated to me.

But then, being more competitive than shy—or maybe having too many fat cells where my brain should be—when my sister-in-law announced she would take the advancement tests, I decided I would too. Hey, even a five-year old could do it, right?

Much to my surprise I advanced, and that victory gave me confidence. When it came time to sign the children up for the next tournament, still on my low-blue-belt high, I inked up as well.

My biggest fear about fighting in a tournament, other than getting the snot slapped out of me, was getting the snot slapped out of me by my sister-in-law. I love her dearly, but I would never want her to lay a smack down on me—she's pretty tough.

Fortunately for me, I outweighed her by two stone (you'll have to figure out just how much that is), which put me in a different weight division than my sister-in-law, so she smacked around a much smaller person than me. With only two women in the "Large Marge" division, I instantly became a medal contender, and ended up winning two medals. It sounds even better when you don't divulge the number of competitors in your division, but I have disclosure and broadcast issues!

We became identified as the "karate" family. It was kind of fun to be recognized as such, and I really enjoyed the level of family participation.

It wasn't all glory and medals, though. Our sensei taught us—drilled it into us—that we were never to use karate as a weapon against others; we were to use it only in self-defense. He emphasized discipline and respect. I also threatened my children to never use their karate training against other children, even if they were "just messing around."

We got a call from my son's first-grade teacher, notifying us that our son had "used karate" on another child. She told us if it happened again, he could be suspended. We tried to keep from laughing, because this was the child who sparred with his cousin and never made contact with punches or kicks.

Of course, we didn't laugh to her face or his. Instead, we asked for his side of the story. It turns out that another child was kicking him, so he blocked the kick. It wouldn't have been a problem, except our son had been bragging to all around that he knew karate.

His defense was to block the kick; the other child's defense was to report the little braggart to the teacher. We tattled to his sensei. I'm happy to say that if he used karate again in school, we didn't hear about it.

My son wasn't the only one to get carried away with karate. My oldest daughter excelled in it. She was small for her age and seemed to surprise the judges with her form and precision.

She did well in class and competition. There weren't a lot of competitive events where we lived, so we enrolled in all there were. On the morning of one event, she complained about feeling sick. She had a sore throat and a slight fever but, with a little prodding from me and a dose of ibuprofen, she agreed to compete anyway.

The pain reliever brought her fever down, and she made it through kata, or forms, just fine. When her turn for kumite, or sparring, came around, she could barely drag herself on to the mat to face her opponent.

Her opponent immediately scored a point, barely making contact, but my daughter collapsed to the floor. The paramedic on duty rushed out to help her, and the poor girl who was sparring with my daughter felt horrible. I felt pretty bad myself, but not as bad as my daughter, who was quite sick.

After the tournament, we took my daughter to the urgent care to find out she had strep throat. I felt like a terrible mom. It took me longer to get over the guilt than it took her to get over the strep. I hope the young lady who thought she made my daughter collapse got over the trauma of decking a tiny little blonde girl.

As time passed, my children got tired of the practice, the tournaments, and karate in general. I tried to push them to continue, but my husband gently reminded me I shouldn't use karate as a weapon. I didn't want him to report me to my sensei, so I backed off.

We decided to quit taking karate classes. Because we didn't all achieve the highest rank of black belt, I privately felt like we were "quitters." It took a few years for me to get over that feeling. My children are better learners than I am because they were soon able to move on and let it go.

It took a wise counselor to help me see that just because we were once a "karate" family, it didn't mean that we always had to define ourselves that way. Seasons change, people change, and circumstances change. Even that first-grade teacher changed—her name, when she got married. I would have recommended changing the white-gray Cruella De Vil streak in her hair—but, hey that's just me.

The one thing that hasn't changed is that my son still uses karate when I try to punch him. He's much bigger than I am now, and he blocks hard. My husband tells me to stop trying to spar with him, but I can't resist. So my husband stands by as we jab, block, and kick and hopes he won't have to call the paramedics. The sensei changed his number.

Lake Powell . . .

Big L, Little L,
Lovely, lazy lake,
Outdoor recreation is
Sometimes hard to take.

Sometimes older children complain about the privileges enjoyed by the younger children once the older ones are grown and out of the nest. It's too bad they don't keep a list of the things they are thankful they didn't have to endure when they were growing up.

Take, for instance, our annual Lake Powell trip. These adventures officially began when it was just our youngest three children around to enjoy them. That was about the time we bought our first boat, which was old, faded, and barely floated—a lot like me.

My husband was a huge fan of boating. I wanted to be, but I had one little problem: I was afraid of water and couldn't really swim. As a teenager, I kind of taught myself how to swim, so I can swim about four feet now, but since most boats don't sink four feet from shore, I can't really count on that skill.

I was determined to like boating, and once I learned that my life jacket really would keep me afloat, the next obstacle I faced was how to hoist my carcass back on the boat if I happened to fall into the water. My husband introduced me to the swim ladder, so another excuse was taken away from me.

My husband gallantly gave me the option of backing the Suburban and boat down the long ramp or boarding the boat, backing it off the trailer, and pulling over to the dock. I trust terra firma much more than the great deep, so I had to learn to back down the ramp. If the ramp was, say, eight lanes wide, I could do it—providing there were no other boaters wishing to use the ramp for thirty minutes. I gave thanks that my husband—and the other boaters—kept their thoughts to themselves.

One attempt to launch the boat on a ramp that was only three or four lanes wide and rather short caused me severe stress. It was a busy boating day, and I had to actually stick to the one lane I was allotted. After several failed attempts to back down the ramp, a young man, who was either extremely sympathetic or just wanted to launch his own boat before sundown, carefully approached me and offered assistance.

He taught me a trick to backing up with a trailer attached—simply place your hand on the bottom of the steering wheel, and whatever direction you want the trailer to go, that's the direction you move your hand (you have to actually keep your hand on the steering wheel, though). Oh yeah—and go slow, and be patient. The patient part was contrary to my nature, but embarrassment and a desire to conquer the art of boat launching won out. I learned to launch a boat using only a couple of lanes at a time. I was ready to become an avid boater.

My husband had fond memories of camping at Lake Powell as a youth. My own memories of camping consisted of the few times he and I had taken the kids into the woods, hunkered down in our tent, and waited for the rain to stop. Oh, and there was that one really fun time when our son, who was a very deep sleeper, got out of his sleeping bag and walked over and peed on us.

My dear hubby assured me it rarely rained at Lake Powell and our boat had a head ("head" is a technical term meaning "port-a-potty wedged in a teeny-tiny space and smells like a teeny-tiny outhouse") so I agreed to go.

Several of the trips blur together, which I believe is a kind blessing from our Maker. Some memories stay etched in my mind, and will probably stay there until my mind goes completely.

Like the time we found a camping spot on a sandstone hill that had approximately seven square inches of sandy beach at the base. Unable to anchor the tent pegs into the ground and learning that the wind doth blow at Lake Powell, we searched for a means of securing our tent. We decided that big stones should be sufficient, so we sent our children out to search for some.

Eager to obey, they hurried off to find rocks that would be big enough. They worked together to find the perfect rock, and when they found a nice big one that they could move together, they bent down to move it as a team. In unison, they let out a scream that sounded something like "SNAKE!!!"

They ran back to where we were setting up the tent and told us that not only had they seen a snake, but they had heard it rattle. My husband went to investigate and took a shovel with him—I guessed to bury the body (I hoped it would be the snake's body and not one of the kids'). A two-foot rattler is no match against my husband and his trusty shovel. He returned a few minutes later, with all children accounted for, to announce that one less rattlesnake graced the world.

I then announced that there would be one less tent gracing the sandstone—we were sleeping on the boat. Six of us managed to sleep on the boat that night. It was cozy, and it was hot; until the next morning when it was cozy and wet, because—you guessed it—it rained at Lake Powell.

I am a good-natured soul if I can get my carbonated beverage (and I did) and if the sky clears (and it did), so we put away the wet things and decided to have a fun day in the water. We inflated the tube, piled the children on it, and began our fun-filled day. A few minutes into the fun-fest, the boat died. My husband, who is a much better mechanic than he is a weather forecaster, narrowed the problem down to a couple of possibilities—both of which required parts we didn't have.

One thing I quickly learned about boating is when you pass a stranded boater, you should offer help because it could easily be you the next time. Most boaters operate by this code of honor, or should I say "code of been there," so all we had to do was wait for someone to pass. Cell phones get no reception in the remote areas, and our boat radio had died long before the boat itself did.

A friendly neighborhood cliff-diver was the first one to

come by and stop. We asked him to send out a tow boat when he got to the marina, but he offered to take my husband there and back to get the needed part. He towed us back to our campsite where the children played in the water while I found some shade and another cold beverage.

Several hours and two hitch-hiking episodes later, my husband returned with the part. He quickly put it on and voila! It did not fix the problem. Turns out it was the other possibility.

Discouraged, we considered our options:

A) have someone tow the boat back to the boat ramp, or,
B) live with the rattlesnakes for the rest of our short, short lives.

I prayed for inspiration and then felt like I should try to start the boat again. It started! I called to my husband and we feverishly packed up camp, hoping to make it back to the marina before the boat died again. As we loaded the last of our belongings, the engine sputtered and died.

When I'd heard the boat start, I'd felt like my prayer was answered. When I heard it die, I remembered that reception isn't that good in some of those remote spots. Or perhaps I should have been more specific in my prayers—after all, the boat did start; I was the one who failed to specify how long I wanted it to keep running.

Our cliff-diving friend stopped by camp again and offered to tow us in if we paid for gas money.

It took us a few hours to get back to the boat ramp, where we roped the boat onto the trailer. One reason it took so long was the captain of our rescue boat, who swilled beer faster than a boat sucks up gas, had to stop and "check the prop" about every twenty minutes. ("Check the prop" is a technical term for peeing in the lake). I guess he didn't have a head on his boat.

Our children had a great time diving in the lake every time the boats stopped. When my husband and I joined them, we discovered we could still have fun, even though our vacation was abruptly cut short.

We took the rattle from the dead snake as a souvenir, and when I showed it to my cub scouts they were unimpressed, having all seen, wrestled, or bred snakes that were much bigger than the one my husband shoveled to death.

On a different trip, we had a flat tire before we even left, which my husband took down and got repaired. Several miles later another tire blew, so we traveled the rest of the way without a spare. As we pulled out of the water, we could hear another tire leaking air, so we ended up replacing all four trailer tires that trip.

Our boat didn't break down that year, but our friend's boat ran out of gas, so we towed him back to the marina, which was closed by the time we got there, shortly after the sun had dropped below the horizon. We headed for the launch ramp, about a mile away, but our boat ran out of gas halfway there. We sat in the dark, in two disabled boats, with the wind blowing us toward the rocks.

We yelled to the houseboats moored across the channel, but they couldn't hear us. Finally our daughter, our friend, and our friend's daughter swam across the channel to beg gas from a house boat.

It seems evident to me that camping just isn't my thing,

although my husband and most of my children love it. I finally convinced them to let me plan the camping trip one year. My idea of camping was booking a condo in Park City. It was wonderful to relax by the pool, shower every day, and eat at restaurants every night. Some people might say we weren't really roughing it—but, trust me, we were. There were no cabana boys or room service.

We've now combined the best of both worlds—we take our trip to Lake Powell each year, but we stay in a hotel in a town just past Glen Canyon Dam and dine out every night. There are still no cabana boys (we have Cancun for that), and some sort of adventure awaits us each year, like finding the homeless person who lived in the bushes outside the hotel. And, of course, there are lots of "dam" jokes.

A friend of ours pointed out that family boating trips provide parents with an opportunity to have their children as "captive" audiences for a few hours. It's true; some great discussions have come about while we were on the lake. Such as "Who wants to swim across the channel in the dark and beg for gas?" or "You flag the next boat down, I'm tired of waving the oar."

I recently suggested we make camping at Lake Powell an annual Ferran Clan event—a traditional family get-together with all six of our children and their children.

My three oldest ones enthusiastically agreed—they apparently have short memories. The three youngest ones are still "captive" and can't say no. I think they may be quietly cheering that there will be more snake-killers and channel-swimmers to help them next year.

# **M**eals . . .

Big M, Little M,
My picky-ness just might,
Make our meals monotonous,
Paranoia is my plight.

One of the toughest questions I have to answer every single day of my life is one that women everywhere can identify with: "What's for dinner?"

As if it's not bad enough that we have asked ourselves this question several times during the day, we have to listen as each member of our family returns home with the very same query.

If I were an organized person, I could make menus in advance, shop from my list, and only face this problem once a week. Either my organizational skills are lacking or my attention span is. Hold on, I just saw a Hershey's Kiss under the chair. Mmmm.

Anyway, I'm pretty certain I'm not an organized person. I have met only a few people who are that organized, and to those of you who are—great job!

The few times I have tried to organize my method for

determining what's for dinner, it has lasted a week or two before I run out of time, patience, or both, and it's back to winging it.

At my house, the dinner dilemma is complicated by picky eaters. I know most people have a picky child or two; in my case, I am the picky eater. I have issues with anything that contains vinegar—which rules out most condiments and salad dressings.

Pickles are the worst. They are banned from my house. To the dismay of my children, I hate pickles in all forms (except in their original state as cucumbers on the vine). No pickles defile my refrigerator or pantry shelves. If a food could be my nemesis—pickles would be it.

Since I've forced my children to resort to beggary from neighbors and friends when they crave pickles, they have started using pickles as a form of torture to get back at me. When we walk by pickle displays at the store, a child will always point out that they know I want some. My teenage daughter recently came home with a picture on her phone of the perfect gift for me—a pickle game (she dodged before I could smack her). Then there was the Christmas one child gave the other children a jar of pickles as a present, thinking I couldn't thwart gift-giving. But mothers reserve the right of veto when it comes to pickles and hamsters—even when they are cleverly disguised as gifts.

Aside from not liking pickles, I have texture issues and chunk phobias. If I can't identify it, I can't eat it. Many things I can identify, I can't eat. Mushrooms, onions, and peppers fall into the "yuck" category for me. That means a lot of sauces are out.

I also have a very sensitive sense of smell. I blame that sensitivity for being the source of disliking so many things because I just can't get past the nasty odors (such is the basis of the vinegar ban). One day, I smelled pickles on our telephone and identified the culprit as a ten-year-old neighbor girl who had consumed one before she came over. I introduced her to Mr. Disinfectant, and she and he got to know each other on my phone as she listened to the "never use my phone if you have eaten pickles because I can always smell it" lecture.

Perhaps you know someone who is as picky as I am; if so, I am sorry. I'm sure it is difficult to live with.

At this point you may be thinking, "What's wrong with this woman is no small thing." I can't deny that. Or perhaps you fear for my children's health—physical and mental. They are healthy in spite of my influence, but they do claim that they may need therapy later on. Maybe you're thinking, "What does that poor woman eat? She must be skinny as a rail." I assure you, I have never been mistaken for being thin. I apparently have NO issues with chocolate or sugar, especially if they are combined with butter.

Because I am so picky, I think my children shouldn't be pickier than I am. I've already ruled out a lot of foods, so it seems to me that they could at least like the things I like. Not so.

It's almost as if they're individuals! They each have their own likes and dislikes, although some, like my oldest daughter, will eat just about anything. When she invites me to her home now, she apologizes for all the food in her house that may gross me out.

Another one of my children is ultra-picky. In addition to hating almost all of the things I hate, he refuses to eat chicken, pork, or peanut butter. I don't know why he has an aversion to chicken and pork, but the peanut butter ban stems from an article he read about how many insect parts there are in every jar. The insect parts don't bother me; I figure they're just a little bonus protein. I can't see them, smell them, or crunch them, so I can ignore them. (Well, crunchy peanut butter does crunch, so I just try not to think about whether it's peanuts or tiny insect exoskeletons.)

Because several of us are so finicky, our menus are quite limited. So when the dinner question gets asked and I answer it, I'm always greeted by groans and complaints. I hear something like "I don't like that," or "I'm sick of that, we always have that." (Although, I'd like to know what's wrong with pizza five nights a week.)

One solution that has worked for me was born out of desperation. Coming home from work physically and mentally exhausted, I knew something had to give, and I also knew the likelihood of a chief cook and bottle washer dropping from the sky was a bit slim. So, out of desperation, we decided to assign meal nights to the children; not necessarily a novel idea, but one we had yet to try.

My children ranged from six to fifteen at the time. I knew inside that I really should train them how to cook the assigned dinner, but that was beyond me at that point—and it also might have involved me having to touch an ingredient I didn't like. So we simply assigned each person a weeknight that became their night to choose dinner.

They had to choose under the following restrictions:

1. No ordering out.
2. We had to have the ingredients on hand.
3. You couldn't complain about anyone else's choice on their night to choose.

Although I still had to cook the meal, I was astounded at how much easier it was when I didn't have to decide on the meal myself. My children discovered that it wasn't easy to come up with an idea for dinner. Of course, we had a few nights when one person just couldn't face the dinner chosen by his sibling, and on those "I just can't stand it" nights, the picky person was allowed to have a sandwich.

I wish I could say it broadened our palettes, but it didn't. We were still stuck in the same menu-option rut, but the pressure of deciding was now spread among the ranks.

After I quit work, we drifted back to the old ways of Mom deciding the dinner. Without all my creativity having been sucked from my brain during a full day at the office, I became a little more experimental. I actually discovered I liked cooking when I wasn't so drained from working.

To my husband's astonishment, I made fajitas one evening—complete with peppers and onions. My children almost jumped for joy when they came home to find ketchup in the refrigerator. Our house had been a Condiment-Free Zone for so long. I finally caved in and started buying mayonnaise and ranch dressing, as long as my children promised to rinse off the dishes after they used either of them and to never, ever mix them. I still couldn't eat those things, but allowing them in the house was a major step forward.

Then came the day when I sautéed onions with ground beef! I made guacamole one night and even ate some (before the green chiles were added—I'm not super-human). A strange miracle was working in our household. My narrow mind was opening—at least a crack.

My ultra-picky son still claims he won't eat peanut butter, but he did confess that he ate chicken at his girlfriend's house the other day. Hmmm, I wonder if he would eat insect parts for her. Well, if he does, he can chase it down with ketchup or mayo—I now have both. Just don't ask me to touch them or smell them.

oses . . .

Big N, Little N,
What begins with those?
Not another earthquake!
No, it's Dad blowing his nose!

Noses are interesting things. You can put them in other people's business, get them out of joint, pick them, or even scare the neighbor's children—or the neighborhood at large—with them.

My husband falls into the latter category. He is neither loud spoken nor ill-mannered. He cringes when he has to dine with the rest of the family, especially in public, because he doesn't belch loudly, reach across others for his food, gulp his drinks, or use dinner rolls as dress shields.

You can be tricked into believing he is quiet, and he is, for the most part. However, when he blows his nose, there is a resonance that reverberates throughout the room, house, and neighborhood that prompts you to duck, drop, and take cover.

He doesn't do this on purpose. He has had surgery to correct his deviated septum and suffers from many allergies.

We've grown accustomed to the sound and hardly notice it anymore; much like when you live next to an airport, you get used to the sound of huge jumbo jets landing and taking off.

We are jolted back to the reality of the noise when a new friend is over visiting, especially one of my children's friends. Adults try to ignore the noise, although they are visibly startled by the trumpeting. Children rarely hold back. After the initial bolt or cringe, they say, "WHAT was that?" My children, who are oblivious to it by now, reply, "What was what?"

"That noise! Didn't you hear it?" As our child tries to figure out what the friend is talking about, they usually hear the second round of blowing. They try to calm their friend. "That's just my Dad blowing his nose."

The friend may appear to be reassured, but when my husband comes back into the room, the friend is careful to avoid him. We've considered having him greet our daughters' dates with a good nose-blowing rather than by coolly cleaning a shotgun in their presence.

It is amazing how we can become accustomed to most things. When we are around something long enough, we just consider it normal. Sometimes we even adopt the behavior ourselves. I believe I blow my nose much louder than most people, simply because by comparison, I am still much quieter than my husband—and he is the nose-blowing measuring stick I am around the most.

Come to think of it, my husband's driving has rubbed off on me as well. He drives fast. When he takes a neighbor or friend to the airport, they grip their seat white-knuckled, relief evident when they are able to board a slower-moving craft—the airplane.

I am a calm, slower driver. At least I thought I was. Then I heard my friends describe how fast I drive and realized I was only calm and slow compared to my driving measuring stick—my dear husband. Maybe there is a reason our nick-names for each other when we were dating were the names of race car drivers.

Now we're reaping what we've sown. As our children learn to drive, they point out all of the minor infractions we make, such as rolling through a stop sign, not signaling when we turn, or stopping too close to another vehicle at a light. When we complain that they're speeding, they point out that Dad and I both do it. They probably think it's okay to blow your nose really, really loudly too.

Speaking of noses, they can also be a source of concern (to girls especially) as they pertain to your looks. When you consider the fact that noses are smelling organs that poke out of the center of your face, you really shouldn't expect them to be a source of aesthetic beauty. But we do. And they aren't.

One of my earliest and longest-lasting mental scars occurred because of my nose. I was twelve years old and I heard my older brother's friend say to him, in reference to me, "How many times has her nose been broken?"

The fact that I was twelve and had a slight crush on the guy made it worse. Having never worried about my nose being big and misshapen, I was suddenly convinced that my nose was horrible. I spent hours looking at it in mirrors from every angle, stressing over the large lump that, in my mind and mirror, resembled a ski jump.

Fortunately for me, when I was seventeen I was in a car accident that resulted in my nose actually being broken. In my opinion, it was a vast improvement. I took another blow to the nose when I was playing basketball with my children, and my son's head provided another impromptu nose job.

I think my nose looks so much better now than it did when I was twelve years old. Maybe it's because the two accidents really did straighten it out, or perhaps my head has just grown into my nose. Then again, it could be that my nose looks pretty good, by comparison, poking out there between the wrinkles. At any rate, I *believe* it looks better; therefore, it *is* better.

My husband also believes he doesn't blow his nose that loudly, but that doesn't make it so. I know he's just a little hard of hearing, so I'll let him live in his world of self-delusion. It helps that I live there with him.

Overreacting . . .

O can be objective,
Unless you have to say,
Oh, our mom is overreacting,
In her opinionated way!

I think it is safe to say that, as parents, most of us want our children to grow up to be law-abiding, well-mannered, respectful citizens. I feel safe using that generalization since I've never met a parent who encouraged his or her child to be a belching, belligerent felon; although many of us have feared that very outcome when faced with certain behaviors.

Our oldest children tend to be the recipients of our uptight paranoia. They are the ones on whom we practice, attempting to hone our parenting skills in hopes of creating viable contributors to society.

As first-time parents, we have plenty of opinions about what is best for our child and often don't like our own well-meaning parents to offer advice. After all, the world has changed since the Stone Age. Our parents used let us ride in autos unrestrained by seat belts or car seats and even let us ride in the back of pickup trucks. We walked most places alone, and they even dipped our pacifiers in honey.

Parents tend to overreact with their first-born. Sometimes we overreact with our second-born, third-born, and so on, but I think it's more common that we tend to relax a little more with each subsequent child.

Our younger children seem to get more free rein—whether it's because we've learned something about parenting or because we're just old and worn out is still unclear. Perhaps it's because we've realized that the law of diminishing returns applies to our efforts with our children as well as economics.

The results of my overreacting to my older children's antics can still be seen today. Or rather, heard—they love to remind me of the injustices I heaped upon them when they were young. At the time, I felt my opinions were quite justified. Today, I think I may have overreacted.

Many, many years ago (not to be confused with "Long, long ago when dinosaurs roamed the earth"), my husband and I were struggling with a new business. We worked long hours at an existing business as well as the new one. We also had two small children, and the hours we worked weren't always conducive to finding a sitter.

Luckily, the new business didn't take up the entire leased space. There was a narrow, adjacent room that my two children, ages three and four, could play in while we worked.

We took toys for them to play with and checked on them quite regularly. The area that connected the two spaces was in the back, out of the customer's view. We strictly admonished them not to come around to the front—unless it was an emergency.

They played quite happily, refrained from emerging into the customer area, and stayed out of mischief—for the most part.

One evening, when I went back to check on them, I noticed they had been playing with an insulated cooler we had left in the back. I wasn't concerned at first; after all, they hadn't shut each other inside the cooler, and all appeared fine—until I looked inside.

Someone had used the cooler as a urinal! I was appalled and demanded to know which one of them did it. They giggled and admitted they each took a turn. I was even more disgusted because the bathroom was just a few steps away. Why would they do such a thing?

They had no explanation for their behavior and tried to look repentant—as much as a three- or four-year-old can look repentant. I informed my husband, who was as revolted as I was. Had we raised animals?

We proceeded to lecture them about acting like animals, not humans. Although looking back, if we had ever owned an animal that was disciplined or talented enough to urinate in a cooler, we may have been more enthusiastic pet owners.

As we made the fifteen-minute trip home, we told them that if they wanted to act like animals, we had no choice but to treat them as such. We explained that animals were not allowed inside our house, so they would have to stay outside once we arrived home.

We pulled in the driveway, unbuckled them from their car seats (hey—we were concerned about their safety, after all), and opened the gate to the backyard. When they protested,

I said, "I'm sorry. You chose to act like animals and we keep animals in the back yard, so that's where you have to go."

They weren't too concerned and went off to play in the back yard. My husband and I went inside through the house to check on them. In our defense, we lived in a quiet neighborhood in southern California and the weather was balmy.

We had a large sun porch located off the kitchen, so we stepped out and called them in to the porch. "We let animals come in to the sun porch," we explained. I fixed dinner, opened the sliding glass windows, and called my offspring to dinner.

I handed them their macaroni and cheese through the window, setting it down on the floor. My husband and I sat at the kitchen table eating our dinner, watching our little ones eat their food on the floor of the sun room. They thought it was fun and ate like animals.

After dinner, they asked to come inside a time or two; we reminded them that animals stayed outside. Being children, they played the game, amusing themselves.

As it grew dark, we turned the lights on in the sun room and brought out their little Fisher Price sleeping bags. We spread them out on the floor. At this point they really wanted to come inside. Although we were weakening, we insisted that animals couldn't sleep inside. We agreed to keep the light on for them and promised them that we would watch over them.

They snuggled their little bodies down inside their sleeping bags, and accepted the pronouncement. It took about five minutes before my hard heart was softened, and I figured they had learned their lesson about peeing in a cooler.

I asked them if they learned anything from it and, with

some coaching from me, they promised to never pee in a cooler again. I asked them if they wanted to come inside and sleep like children or stay out and sleep like animals. They both wanted to come inside.

At that time, as a young mother, I thought the punishment fit the crime. They never urinated in a cooler again. Looking back, I think maybe I overreacted. Okay, I'm sure I did. The entire time we treated them like animals amounted to about two hours. They were constantly supervised, which is more than I can say about any real animals we ever owned. (And it's more than I can say about my two little children during the day when they were left to play on their own and devise unusual areas to pee in.)

We realized that they had actually acted their age. We wanted them to act like adults—well, adults with good bathroom habits. You would think I'd learn from that experience. Apparently I am a slow learner.

Fast forward five years. Same two children, now ages eight and nine. These two were the owners of two Cabbage Patch Kids named Kasha and Angelique. They had received these Cabbage Patch Kids as a gifts at about the same time they were peeing in coolers.

But now that they were older, they no longer played with Kasha and Angelique. Kasha usually could be found in the bottom of a toy box, his crooked crew cut still showing evidence of his hair melting when he fell against a heater, and Angelique resided on my daughter's bed.

Our child-care provider was a wonderful lady who watched children in her home. My children liked her, and she watched my then-youngest child, who was three, every day. She had the two older ones only when they were "off-track," which was their school's term for one of the three-week breaks they got while attending year-round school.

These older two were old enough to be bored when they were off-track. They thought they were too old for day care, yet they were too young to be left home alone. There were a couple of other elementary-age children that were there too, being off-track as well.

One day, when I came to pick them up, I was informed by the sitter that my two oldest children had been up to mischief that day—very disturbing mischief indeed. They had participated in the dismemberment of a Cabbage Patch Kid that belonged to one of the other girls who was off-track. The three of them had torn the Cabbage Patch Kid limb from limb.

Rational thinking halted and overreaction kicked in. I had visions of two hoodlums, disrespecting property and disregarding the basic rights of Cabbage Patch Kids and their owners everywhere. I apologized to the sitter and assured her I would talk to my children.

Talking, lecturing—I get the two confused. I talked—my children say I lectured—most of the twenty-minute drive home. I determined that for destroying another child's toy, my children would have to replace it with a new one, with their own money. This brought up protests: the doll they destroyed was old, why should they have to buy a new one, the girl didn't even like it anymore, blah, blah, blah.

Then I told them the second part of the punishment—because they were so disrespectful in their destruction, they would each have to give up their own Cabbage Patch Kid to the girl whose doll was ruined. This pronouncement brought even greater protests, at least from my daughter. Why should that girl get three dolls when she didn't even want her own doll? My son didn't care much about his doll (Kasha); he was more concerned about the money he had to give up to buy a new doll.

Their protests told me I had found an effective punishment. They had to carry through with buying a new doll and giving up their own dolls. They never dismembered another Cabbage Patch Kid—or anything else, to my knowledge— ever again. I felt the punishment fit the crime.

My son pretty much forgot about it and let it go. My daughter, on the other hand, has never forgotten about Angelique and the injustice of it all. She still gets fired up when we talk about it. I finally asked her why she was so upset—it happened years and years ago, and the punishment was effective.

She told me that the young owner of the torn-up doll was actually the instigator of the crime in the first place. My daughter and son had joined in only after the girl had started the destruction on her own. It took me years to actually listen to that part. I was so caught up in making sure my children didn't get away with a rampant act of hooliganism that I didn't listen to what their roles actually were. I overreacted.

I can't bring back the lost Cabbage Patch Kids. I can't retract putting the little "animals" out on the sun porch. I can try to listen a little better and impress upon my younger children how lucky they are that I am a lot less uptight and a lot more tired these days. I don't have the energy to overreact—as much.

I can also chuckle as I watch my daughter, a first-time parent, try to fit the punishment to the crime as her little daughter gets into all sorts of mischief. I think it's so much cuter now that it's my grandchild instead of my child. Objectively speaking, of course.

Pets . . .

Pleading for a puppy,
Pestering for a cat,
Bunnies, birds, and guppies,
Prohibited per contract.

I am pleased to announce that my household is one without pets. My husband and I are the proud owners of a contract, signed by my children, agreeing to no more pets.

There was a time when we could not make this claim to fame. Over the years, we have been the owners of four dogs, a cat, two turtles, two budgerigars, a Jenday conure, numerous beta and koi fish, and . . . one flop-eared bunny.

The bunny was the proverbial last straw. The bunny was to blame for the evil genius of getting the children to stop begging for pets.

The bunny hopped into our garage one afternoon. It was a soft, flop-eared, lovable little creature that immediately caused my children to melt into whining puddles of "Mom, can we keep it? Mom, can we pleeeease keep it?"

At the time, we had two dogs, a cat, two budgies, several fish, and the Jenday conure. We also had three children and two adults who had tested positive for allergies to dogs, cats, and birds. The five of us traveled to the allergy clinic weekly to receive injections, in hopes of becoming immune to the critters.

I do have to mention at this point that neither my husband nor I even wanted one pet. We had no desire to be pet owners. Like many parents, our current menagerie was the result of indulging our children. Also like many parents, we ended up either nagging our children to care for the pets or doing it ourselves.

I digress—back to the story. I had no intention of becoming the owner of a bunny. I quickly pointed out to my children that a bunny as fine as that one must have an owner who would be looking for it. It certainly didn't look like a street bunny or just any wild hare.

My children volunteered to take the bunny door-to-door in an effort to find its owner. I smiled as they went on their quest, certain that they would come home without "Jazzrabbit."

I should have recognized the warning sign—the fact that they had named the bunny. That clue should have led me to the conclusion that my kids would happily traipse home with "Jazzrabbit." I didn't figure it out until they came back, tired yet triumphant.

"Nobody owns him! Can we keep him? Pleeeease?" I tried logic on them. I wanted to know where they would keep him, what they would feed him, what they would do if the dogs got him, and how they would feel when the owner eventually surfaced to claim the bunny.

They had evidently been plotting as they were going door-to-door looking for the owner. They had a friend with an extra rabbit cage, and my daughter volunteered to purchase the food and other bunny necessities. They topped off their argument with, "We know the owner will find him eventually, we just can't let him wander around, cold and hungry. We'll give him back when the owner shows up."

I pointed out that a bunny doesn't do well caged up all the time, and my daughter offered to take him on daily walks. I explained that you can't walk a bunny like a dog and protested that nobody even walked the dogs (which were very walkable, if you didn't mind being dragged down the sidewalk by the big one).

They continued to hound me about the bunny. I reminded them that their dad and I didn't even like animals. They promised to do all the work. I'd heard it all before. Suddenly, I had an idea. I asked them how badly they wanted the bunny. They assured me they wanted this bunny more than any other pet.

Then I presented the deal: they could keep the bunny if they would promise to never ask for another pet again. They were experiencing bunny love and readily agreed to it. I'm sure they figured when the time came for another pet, they could weasel one out of me. It had worked several times before.

So I struck a bargain with them: they would sign a contract, in writing, that stated that in exchange for the bunny, they agreed to no more pets—period. They figured they had nothing to lose. They already had dogs, a cat, birds, and fish. Why would they want another pet? They agreed to sign.

So we ended up with the cage from the friend who happened

to have an empty one (mighty coincidental, I thought), cedar shavings to line the cage, a bag of rabbit food, and—I am not making this up—a ferret harness.

The ferret harness was an idea that seized my daughter while we were at the pet store. She could take the bunny for walks with one of those handy harnesses and a leash. So the fat little bunny body got stuffed into the ferret harness, or at least the top part of the ferret harness, because a bunny is a bit plumper than a ferret.

She hooked on the leash and took Jazzrabbit out for a walk. I am assuming, for purposes of this story, that Jazzrabbit was a "he" and not a "she." I really never knew, nor cared to know. He hopped under a bush and crouched there for several minutes until my daughter got bored and dragged him out from under the bush. She unhooked the leash, and put Jazzrabbit back into the cage, still in his ferret harness.

Meanwhile, I went to the computer and drew up a contract stating that in consideration of being allowed to keep the bunny, the children agreed to no more pets. I used mighty fine legalese and printed it out, complete with places for all of us to sign.

Luckily, they signed before the glow of the new bunny had worn off, which was approximately the next morning when we discovered Jazzrabbit had chewed through his ferret harness. He had also reached up through his cage to the brand new snow pants hanging on the hooks above, dragged one pant leg into his cage, and chewed several holes in it.

He couldn't be trusted outside without his leash and harness, so he sat in his cage getting fatter and fatter. His claws grew long from lack of exercise, and I wondered if I should set him free. My children didn't want him to face the harsh winter and they didn't like my jokes about rabbit tasting just like chicken, either.

No one ever came to claim Jazzrabbit. I wished we hadn't claimed him either. My consolation was the No More Pets contract. I would take it out to read it sometimes, as a comfort, and to revel in the knowledge that someday we would be a pet-free household.

The bunny disappeared one day, cage and all. It was the same day that Jackson, the incontinent cocker spaniel, disappeared. My husband and I had an arrangement, you see. I allowed the pets in the first place, and he had to make other living arrangements for them, when the time came. It wasn't really a formal arrangement, it was more of an I'll-do-something-about-it-so-you'll-finally-stop-your-complaining sort of agreement. It worked.

I was the soft parent, giving in to the demands of my children. He was the tough parent, cleaning up the messes we left behind (and we really couldn't blame the animals). The only good thing that came out of the bunny fiasco was the No More Pets contract.

We still have the contract, and the pets are all long gone. Some were sold or given away, and others passed on to another realm or were left at the animal shelter.

My three youngest children sometimes complain that the contract shouldn't be binding on them since they were not named parties to the deed. I remind them that they cannot appeal this decision, but when they are eighteen and living on their own, they are welcome to have as many pets as they want. Then I advise them to go play with the neighbor's dog.

Quilts . . .

Big Q, Little Q,
What begins with Q?
A quick queue of quilts,
Qualify as keepsakes too.

A few years ago, I attended a meeting for women at our local church that focused on talents. I'd been to several of these sorts of get-togethers in the past, and while I enjoyed visiting with and getting to know people, I cringed at the thought of trying to display some of my talents. Those refined women didn't seem to be the type to appreciate the fine art of belching loudly.

I procrastinated signing up for a display when, at the last minute, I thought to myself, "Hold on! You do have talents. You've made quilts for your children, you crochet afghans, you scrapbook, you've made pajama pants, even pioneer dresses for a trek—you have a lot to display. Just do it!"

So I did. I took over my armfuls of proof that I had talents. I arranged a spot on one of the display tables, made a little placard with my name on it, and rather proudly set it out. Then I wandered around, looking at the other displays, which were pretty amazing.

I found out a friend of mine made beautiful quilts. Not only did she quilt, instead of tie, these themed masterpieces, they were her original designs, for which she sold the patterns. Did I mention she taught quilting classes in several venues?

Another station showed scrapbooks that were embossed, beribboned, and told a pictorial history of the lives of one woman's six children, from birth to current day.

Professional-looking children's clothing adorned another area, making my homemade pajamas look—homemade!

Several pans full of aromatic, gooey cinnamon rolls displayed another woman's excellent cooking skills.

I felt mediocre. I was the Jack of all trades but master of none. I wanted to gather up my imperfect items and tuck them safely away from ridicule, but I had to content myself with surreptitiously removing my name card from the display.

Later I realized that I was so busy comparing my mediocrity with other people's best that I didn't even realize the only actual ridicule was coming from me. That wasn't celebrating my talents; it was denigrating them. It wasn't constructive; it was destructive.

My homely little quilts, tied with yarn, were made with each of my children in mind. They weren't lacking in any way except professionalism, and maybe my optimistic view of being able to complete three quilts and three afghans by Christmas, when I didn't even start any of them until October.

I made my first quilt when I was fifteen. My home economics teacher showed us how to use quilting frames, tie the quilts, and hand-stitch the hems. Thirty years later, I still have the quilt. It is getting a little threadbare, and I've had to re-stitch the hem, but it's a reminder of one of my earliest domestic accomplishments. At fifteen, it isn't hard to convince yourself you're an expert.

I do have a talent for taking shortcuts. My second quilt was also tied, but was made without the benefit of quilting frames and was hemmed on a sewing machine. I spread it out on the living room floor to tie it. I was eighteen, engaged to be married, and dreaming of the easy, stress-free life to come. (It was a dream; it didn't have to be realistic.) That quilt came out wrinkled with some bumps and lumps in it, much like life turned out to be.

One year, I made quilts for all of my children as Christmas presents. These were made in secret, while they were at school or after they went to bed, and I have a picture of the kids on Christmas Eve, lined up on the couch, each wrapped in his or her personal Mom-made quilt. In the picture, they are all smiling and look like they actually like each other. Some days, that picture is very soothing to me.

Most recently, I switched from quilts to afghans. Crocheting an afghan takes a lot more time than tying a quilt. One advantage of crocheting is you can carry it with you without a lot of concerned looks from others. People tend to look at you strangely when you walk around wrapped in a ragged quilt (although the spare change is nice). I worked on three afghans at once, crocheting one child's afghan in front of the others, being evasive as to whose was whose, so there was some semblance of surprise on Christmas morning.

I worked on one of the afghans during troubling times, as I sat either in counseling or waiting for a child to finish a session of counseling. When that afghan was finished, it became a source of comfort and completion. It was a different kind of therapy, but it helped me as well as the child it was destined for.

Later I learned to combine fleece, batting, and yarn to create "the world's warmest blanket," as proclaimed by my son. He drags it upstairs and downstairs; he sleeps with it spring, summer, fall, and winter—and he is a teenager. I never realized how warm it would make me feel to see him enjoy it so much.

My quilts would never fetch much of a price on the open market, but that's not where they were designed to sell. And my talents might not be worth much out in the world either. But the best measure of their value is what they are worth in my small circle of influence—my family. That's something you can't deposit in the bank or display on a table. And my family can also appreciate my talent for belching. At least the children can. I think my husband would like to remove his name from that display.

ats . . .

Big R, Little R,
Hurrying, scurrying rats,
Rodents running rampant,
One just chased the cat!

One sunny day, near the end of June, I sat outside watching my children splashing in the swimming pool. Our pool was an above-ground unit that was big, rectangular, and four feet deep.

We purchased it one summer when we chose to forgo a family vacation and use the funds to buy a nice swimming pool. The children all saved their money and pitched in to help buy it. It was one of the best investments we ever made. Every summer we had the luxury of swimming when we wanted to, we knew whose pee was in our pool, and with each season, I learned a little more about pool maintenance.

I sat in the shade of our shed, enjoying the day and the sounds of summer. Suddenly, I heard a rustle in the raspberry bushes at the end of the pool, by the shed. I ignored it, but then I heard the sound again. I looked toward the noise and saw some sort of animal there in the greenery.

I glimpsed fur and thought it must be a squirrel, so I called to the kids to get their attention. As I stood up, I startled the creature. I expected it to scurry away, but to my surprise, the "squirrel" jumped, turned 180 degrees, and fled quickly through the plants—but not so quickly that I missed seeing a long, fat, pink tail.

I screeched and asked if anyone else had seen it. I could only describe it as a mouse, only bigger, with a pink tail. My son said one word that made my stomach churn—rat. I admitted it looked like a rat, but since I had never before seen one in real life, I didn't believe an animal that big could be a rat.

We staked out the area, waiting for it to make its appearance when all was quiet. We didn't have long to wait. We heard the rustling again and threw something at the foliage. The varmint scurried away again, but not before we got a good look at it. It was a rat—a big rat.

I ran inside to check on the internet to find out if rats lived in the suburbs. My research confirmed our suspicions. It was definitely a rat.

I was disgusted. I'm not the best housekeeper or yard keeper, but I could not believe we lived in a rat's nest (a pigsty—maybe). My research suggested that there was probably more than one rat. How could this be? Didn't only really dirty, scummy, slummy places have rats?

I read on to find out more. The construction of new homes across the field, the cluttered woodpile at the side of the shed, the open fifty-pound sack of dog food, and the decorative pond in our backyard all combined together to create a giant welcome sign to rat paradise.

My children were intrigued by them. As we examined the shed, inside and out, we saw the evidence of a rat colony. My husband and I discussed the best way to eradicate them. My son ran next door and enlisted the aid of his friends and their pellet guns.

The boys tried to flush the rats out of their burrows and hiding places, eager to shoot one. I drove down to the local IFA to purchase a couple of rat traps and some rat poison.

When I returned home, I went out back to see what the boys were doing. They were nowhere to be found, but there was a dead mouse, sprayed with fluorescent green paint, lying by the shed. It made me shudder—was it a warning left by a giant rat?

When the boys returned, they confessed to leaving the luminescent mouse carcass and I lectured them about the dangers of handling dead rodents, or live ones, for that matter. They assured me that although they were responsible for killing the mouse with a shot from the pellet gun, and did indeed spray the mouse with the paint, they did not touch the mouse. They showed me the tongs they used, and I felt better but gave them one last reminder not to touch a dead mouse or rat. I also made a mental note to buy new tongs. No sense in contaminating perfectly good hot dogs.

Evening came and we placed bits of rat bait around the burrow openings under the shed door. As dusk was beginning to settle in, we borrowed the pellet guns from the neighbor kids again. We couldn't just wait for the poison to do its work; we wanted immediate death to the vermin.

So we sat on chairs, with air rifles cocked, waiting for the curious rodents to peek their heads out. All three of the children were alert, poised to pull the trigger when movement was detected. My husband and I were not immune to the excitement, but it struck me as incredibly funny that we were sitting in the near dark, as a family, shooting rats.

I realized that the strangest things can bring a family together. I handed my borrowed weapon back to my husband and hurried inside to get the camcorder. As I videoed the "hunt," I had to smile. We were intense, we were cheering each other on, and we were united against a common enemy. We were a family.

When one of the children scored a lucky hit, we put down our weapons to examine the trophy. We were disappointed to see it was another mouse. Where was the ugly, massive rat we had seen earlier in the day?

We joked that the rats used the mice as decoys to sniff out danger and find the food. As we laughed at the stupidity of mice, the chunks of rat bait disappeared faster than we could get a shot off. The decoys apparently worked, because we shot no rats that night.

The next day we checked the trap, and a mighty dead rat lay gripped in the jaws of death. We caught a waft of the stench of victory. Unfortunately, the smell of the rats was even stronger. We found evidence of rat tracks all around the shed and knew our problem was much bigger than one creature.

We considered calling an exterminator but were concerned about the expense. A friend recommended a high-frequency transmitter that emitted a sound that was supposed to drive the rats away. We saw no evidence that it worked on rats, although the sound drove *us* away. We were excited when another rat succumbed to the rat trap.

We bought more rat poison, which looked like tasty granola bars. I cautioned my children not to touch the poison, and we kept the dog locked in her kennel. We tried to flood the rats out by turning on the garden hose full force into the burrow. We saw no immediate results, except for providing a swimming hole for them. I also worried that we had given the rats the water reserves they needed so they wouldn't have to emerge from their burrows at all.

As we were about to give up and call an exterminator, the tide turned. It was a sunny morning on the Fourth of July. I walked out in the back yard to check the rat trap. Then I saw it: a dead rat, claws up, there in front of me on the sidewalk. I screeched. I saw another one, closer to the pond. I screeched again.

I grabbed the tongs and the garbage bag to dispose of the bodies. As I looked, I saw more rat bodies. I ran inside to share the news with my family.

We cleaned up twenty-four dead rats that Fourth of July morning. With the two dead rats from the trap and the two dead mice that we shot, that made twenty-eight pieces of vermin removed from our property. It was truly Independence Day for our family. We were free!

After disposing of the carnage, we went to work making our yard the rat anti-paradise. We cleared the woodpile and neatly restacked it. We filled in the burrows around and under the shed. We paid our son to clean out the shed, seal the cracks, and repaint the floor. He accused us of exposing him to hantavirus, but, hey, we paid him fifty bucks and offered him a face mask.

Our family learned a lot from that experience. We hunted together, cleaned together, rejoiced together, and reminded each other to close the lid tight on the brand new dog food container. I even have the video to prove it really happened, except it was too dark to see all of the lawn-chair-sitting, air-gun-toting action. Rats! I guess you'll have to take my word for it.

Singing . . .

Big S, Little S,
Singing's really super,
But your singing is so scary,
That it puts me in a stupor.

There are people who are very musically gifted. There are those who excel at writing and composing music, and those who shine forth through singing. I fit into neither category and it's safe to say that my husband and children are pretty much right there with me.

Our talent lies in appreciating the musical talents of others. We will never be asked to perform in choirs, but we have participated in many an audience. We don't really read music, but we can hear it. Lack of talent has never stopped me from singing around the house, though.

In my early teens, I formed a singing group with my sister and two of our friends. Excited to share our budding talent with others, we recorded a song on a cassette recorder. As we played back the tape for our friends' parents, we eagerly awaited their accolades.

Their response was something like, "It sounds good, but you need to get rid of the person who can't carry a tune." I later learned they meant me.

It stopped me from singing in front of friends or into tape recorders, but it didn't stop me from singing at home or in the car. When I became a mother, I particularly enjoyed singing to my children.

When they were infants, I would sing them a song as I put them down for the night. As they got older, I continued the bedtime ritual when I tucked them in but I let them pick the song. When they couldn't think of one, I would come up with some lyrics hidden in my trivia-filled brain.

In time, they built up a nice little repertoire of songs to choose from. Their choices ranged from "Boom Boom, Ain't it Great to be Crazy?" to "Billy, Don't be a Hero" to "I am Child of God."

I would occasionally get tired of singing every night and convince my husband to take a turn. But then my children complained because he would only sing one song, "Happy Birthday to You," and when they realized it wasn't really their birthday, they quickly lost interest and asked for Mom to sing again.

Their interest was very flattering to my delicate psyche that had been crushed so many years earlier when I had dared to sing on tape. My children assured me that I was a wonderful singer, and I began to believe it must be so.

All good things must come to an end, and my illusion of being a good singer was one of those things. One night, as I went to tuck in my third child, who was about three years old at the time, I asked him what song he wanted to choose.

He didn't want to choose one, so I did. I had just gotten into the song when he placed his little hand over my mouth and said, "Stop." Thinking I had chosen the wrong song, I simply started a different one. Once again his hand covered my mouth as he said, "Stop."

I stopped. I asked him if he wanted me to sing him a different song and he said, "No." I was a little hurt and asked him when I could sing to him again. He looked me in the eye and replied, "Some night. But tonight is not that night." He didn't ask me to sing ever again. It was a little sad for me; I think he was relieved. He stopped having nightmares right about that time. Coincidence?

Since my other children still asked me for songs, I chalked up my son's opinion to bad taste or no taste at all. I kept singing the songs, teaching the lyrics and a love of singing to another generation of individuals who struggled to carry tunes.

Then we got a karaoke machine for Christmas. That in itself was a dangerous gift, but when combined with a video camera, it created the means of producing truly frightening productions that could be played and re-played.

Conveniently forgetting the times I had been gently reminded of my lack of talent, I endeavored to belt out a musical number with my sister-in-law *à la* Whitney Houston. Our spouses thought it would be fun to record it, and we foolishly allowed it.

The only thing worse than hearing a replay of my singing was *watching* and hearing a replay of my singing. Ouch!

I stayed away from the karaoke machine after that, which I suspect was what my husband had in mind when he made the video in the first place. One of my children tripped over the cord of the karaoke machine a few days later, and it crashed to the floor and could not be repaired (at least that's what my husband claimed).

I still sing at home and in the car, usually when nobody else is around. I went through a phase when I would sing and dance (while sitting in the car) as I waited at stoplights, just to see the people around me laugh.

I figured I was doing a good deed, giving people something to smile about. My children had other ideas and begged me to stop.

The child that asked me to stop singing still doesn't like to hear people sing. When my other children or I sing around him, he asks us to stop. I tried to accommodate him at first, but then his attitude started rubbing off on the other children. We got to the point where anytime anyone would sing, someone would ask them to stop.

I finally had to make a new rule. Singing is allowed (except at the dinner table). Singing makes you feel better. It lets you express emotions, and maybe pretend, just for a minute, that you really have talent. I like to hear my family of mediocre singers sing because I know it will improve our moods. We just don't record it or do it in public!

My youngest daughter still asks me to sing. My oldest daughter has started singing songs to my granddaughter at bedtime. The tradition continues, and, who knows? Perhaps our talent will someday evolve, or maybe my children will marry into a musically talented gene pool.

Truth . . .

T, T, T, T
What begins with T?
Telling the truth all the time,
'Til the tale's as tall as me.

I think most parents spend a great deal of time trying to teach their children the importance of always telling the truth. I also believe that children are born with the ability to speak the words that come to their minds—all the words!

We take that talent for telling the truth and try to mold it and shape it; we want them to use judgment in what to blurt out. We wish they would use our judgment.

Many years ago, when my oldest daughter was three, we introduced the subject of death to her. We briefly explained that her Grandpa Joe (my husband's father) and her Grandma Mary (my mother) had died.

She vaguely remembered that Grandma Mary had been very sick before she passed away, but she wanted to know how Grandpa Joe had died. We explained that he had died of a heart attack and that his heart had stopped working.

That explanation seemed to be sufficient for her, and the conversation was forgotten.

Around that same period of time, we were trying to teach her about good health habits. One of the things we talked about was how smoking was bad for your body. She wanted to know why so many people smoked if it was so bad, and we told her that sometimes good people make bad choices. Wanting to give her an example, we used Grandpa Joe, who had been a smoker. We explained that he was a good person; he had just developed a bad habit.

As she was our first child, we were pleased with our frankness and directness in dealing with her questions. We were also clueless as to how a child's mind works. We're still kind of clueless about how a child's mind works, but we're not as proud of ourselves as we used to be.

Needless to say, we soon realized that our three-year old daughter had taken in this new information and was now determined to share it with others. One day we were walking into a store, and she observed a man standing outside the entrance, smoking.

Before I realized what she was doing, she pulled her hand away from mine, marched over to him and informed him in her loud, bossy three-year-old voice, "Smoking is bad! My Grandpa Joe smoked, and he's dead!"

She marched back to us, oblivious of the man's stare. I was too embarrassed to do anything but sweep her into the store. I tried to explain to her how rude she had been, but she didn't understand—after all, she was telling the truth. She felt that man needed to know.

I hoped she would develop prudence in her quest for telling the truth so loudly. But as she got older, I realized that she often felt compelled to share the truth with others—namely me!

When she was about eight years old, I was standing in the kitchen, innocently doing dishes. She wandered in, looked at me for a moment and asked, "Mom, are you embarrassed to go to the store because you're so fat?"

At this point, although I was no Skinny Minnie, it wasn't as if I was big enough to burn diesel and wear mud flaps. Sure, I had an extra twenty pounds that I carried around, but I had just given birth (two years earlier).

I was astounded. Maybe I was fat and just didn't know it. *Should* I be embarrassed to go to the store? I wanted to tell her I was more embarrassed taking her into stores than taking myself because I never knew what she was going to say, but I refrained from voicing my initial thoughts and realized, "Aha, this could be a teaching moment."

I explained to her that I was not fat, although I could stand to lose a few pounds. I gave her a talk about people being different sizes and shapes. I talked about everyone being unique, and that nobody should be so embarrassed about how they looked that it would keep them from going places. I also reminded her that hurtful comments could make someone feel bad.

She endured the mini-lecture and then went on her way to play. I was left in the kitchen wondering just how fat I really was and what diet would get rid of the extra twenty pounds.

It wasn't until much later that I realized there was another teaching moment in that situation. My daughter didn't think I was fat. My daughter thought that I thought I was fat. She had seen me try diet after diet in an effort to get the perfect body and had reached a reasonable conclusion—I must be fat if I was always trying to lose weight. She simply wanted to know if I was embarrassed about it.

My children have never finished educating me with their teaching moments. This same daughter, just a few years ago, spoke the truth to me again at an unexpected moment.

We had recently moved into a new home and were invited to speak in church as a family. We had each worked diligently on our talks, but still felt some nervousness at addressing a congregation full of so many people we didn't know—people who would receive their first impression of our family from what they heard and saw.

As we waited for the meeting to begin, my oldest daughter leaned over to me and whispered, "Mom, you have a mustache." I knew she wasn't talking about a Kool-aid mustache but rather the annoying facial hair that many women are forced to deal with. I think it migrates from my husband's face to mine as we sleep.

It wasn't exactly a news flash to me. It was, however, a really bad time to bring it up. I told her thanks in a sarcastic whisper. She innocently replied, "What? Should I not have said anything?" I shook my head and tried to ignore her.

The meeting was starting and all I could think about was my mustache. If she could see it, could everyone in the congregation see it? Why hadn't I waxed? I could just imagine the whispers: Does she know she has a mustache? Should we leave a bottle of Nair on her doorstep? Which one is the man and which one is the woman?

Needless to say, I was seriously distracted from the spirit of the meeting. As my daughter got up to speak, I silently prayed that she wouldn't announce the presence of my facial hair. She didn't. She did a wonderful job, and I was amazed at her speaking ability. I shouldn't have been—talking is her specialty!

I managed to shake myself out of my facial hair fixation long enough to deliver my talk. As I spoke, I realized that my children were all on the edge of their seats. It occurred to me that they were afraid of the things I might say about them.

I'll admit, in our previous home, when we had been asked to speak in church, I had told an embarrassing tale about each of them. They were true stories, but embarrassing nonetheless. I refrained from doing it that time, perhaps because I was keenly attuned to the true but embarrassing remark my daughter had made to me at the start of the meeting.

I made it through that meeting without frightening anyone with my female mustache. I later drowned my sorrows in a bottle of depilatory. Correction: I drowned the hair in a bottle of depilatory.

I'm still learning about truth and teaching moments. And I still have about twenty pounds I'd like to lose, but I try not to obsess about it. After all, I just had a baby. Twenty years ago. And that's the truth.

Underwear . . .

Big U, Little U,
What begins with U?
Underestimating urchins,
And their underwear too.

When you are a mother employed outside the home, one of the biggest concerns you face is the day care dilemma. Finding quality, affordable day care for your children is an ongoing challenge.

I had friends that I envied because they had mothers or aunts who volunteered to watch their children while they worked. Like most working women, I did not have that option.

There were a few mediocre day care centers I used over the years; a couple that proved to be terrible, prompting quick changes; and a couple of very excellent ones. When you find an excellent day care provider, you tend to put up with rules that may seem overly strict and prices that threaten to break your budget.

Even with the best care providers, parents still worry about their children. When I picked up my children, I paid attention to the atmosphere and demeanor of the children at the center. I also questioned my children on how their day went, what they did, and so on.

One evening, as I was driving home after picking up my then four-year-old son, I asked him about his day.

This was back in the day before passenger-side airbags and their attendant warnings, so he was in the front seat. He sat there in his little camouflage shorts and t-shirt, listening to me talking, when he suddenly interrupted my line of questioning with a loud statement, "I'm not wearing any underwear!"

That got my attention immediately. "What? Where are they?"

He grinned at me, unconcerned, and said, "In my backpack."

"Did you have an accident? Did you wet them?" That was the most obvious reason. I tried to reassure myself.

"No," was his reply.

"Why did you take them off then?" I demanded.

"I wanted to."

Alarmed, I went into a big lecture on why you should not remove your underwear and put them in your backpack and how he was never to do it again. As I ranted at him, I glanced over to make sure the words were sinking in.

He sat there with a big cheesy grin and said, "I'm just kidding, Mom."

"What do you mean? Where are your underwear?"

"I'm wearing them." He still smiled.

"Let me see. Right now!" I reached over and lifted up the leg of his camouflage shorts and, sure enough, his little Batman briefs were right where they belonged—on his body.

Needless to say, I was relieved that the underwear issue was not the problem I thought it might be. However, I was curious to know why he would joke around like that. After several attempts at probing his thought process, his four-year-old mind never came up with a better explanation than, "I was just kidding. I thought it would be funny."

I really cannot blame him, or any of my children, for having such a bizarre sense of humor. They've learned it from me and their father, not to mention the strange genetic mutant humor they were born with.

When my oldest three children were young and still prone to tantrums and pouts that were kind of cute, I used to tease them with the story of their Swamp Parents. I would tell them that their real parents lived in the swamp and had stringy, greasy hair with worms coming out of it. When they whined about our decisions, I offered to let them go back to their Swamp Parents. It didn't take them long to reply that their Swamp Parents were probably an improvement over their dad and me.

I had teased them off and on about their Swamp Parents (always with a smile on my face) over the years, but the joke grew old, even to me, and I stopped doing it.

One afternoon, at the end of a very long week of my husband being out of town, I picked up my children from day care. I was relieved that my husband was on his way home, having felt the heavy responsibility of being the sole parent for too long.

My children had been very good that week, and I took

the opportunity to praise their behavior. I told them, "I am so proud of the way you guys acted this week. It is so hard with Dad gone, and you tried hard not to fight and you really helped me around the house."

My children beamed at my words, so I added a few more. Sometimes I don't know when to quit. "I just want to tell you that your real parents don't live in the swamp. I love you guys so much."

My daughter looked at me with tears in her eyes, "Mom, you're going to make me cry!" She gave a sniff.

I was touched by her emotions. "Why? Because I told you I love you?" I guessed I wasn't verbal enough with telling them how I felt about them and made a mental note to do it more often.

She replied, "No. It's because you finally told us that our real parents don't live in the swamp. You've never told us that before."

I felt terrible. I had teased my children for years about their Swamp Parents and never dreamed they might take it seriously. I couldn't get out the words fast enough. "I am so sorry. I was only teasing when I said your real parents lived in the swamp. Didn't you know that?" I could only imagine what damage I had done to their fragile psyches with my so-called humor.

My daughter laughed and said, "I know that. I was teasing you back! I got you." The children had a good laugh at my expense, which I deserved.

As they have gotten older and developed their sense of humor even more, the children now tend to gang up on their dad and me, and we find ourselves at the butt end of their jokes. I've always taught them not to dish it out if they can't take it, so I try to laugh with them laughing at me. If it gets too bad, I can always go back to my real home—the swamp.

Vacuum Cleaner Salesman . . .

Big V, little V,
Your orange shag carpet room,
Is very, very, very dirty,
And needs a new vacuum.

It was mid-December when our doorbell rang, and I opened the door and my life to the vacuum cleaner salesman. We lived in a small two-bedroom rental apartment with orange shag carpet, where I used to cheer myself with the fact that at least it wasn't *green* shag carpet.

I can't be held entirely to blame for letting him in. It was very cold, and he had a cast on one arm and looked very browbeaten. Still, I could have been strong and turned him away if he hadn't said, "If you just listen to my demonstration, I'll get twenty dollars, and I'll give you this free set of steak knives."

My heart was touched. I could spare a few minutes of my life to listen to this poor man's pitch in order for him to earn twenty bucks. Not to mention, we didn't have any steak knives, and I surely wanted some. It didn't matter that we could never afford to buy steak to cut with those steak knives; it was exciting to have them—just in case.

My husband and I invited him in, and he lugged in the tools of demonstration with him. We reaffirmed that we already had a vacuum cleaner and did not need—and more importantly, could not afford—another one. He assured us he understood and thanked us for allowing him time to demonstrate the vacuum cleaner.

We quickly found out that this was not just a vacuum cleaner. It was a Very Powerful Vacuum cleaner. In the interest of protecting someone's privacy, we'll just call it the VPV. Assembling the VPV was a thing to behold, especially considering the salesman only had limited use of the arm in the cast. My oldest daughter, a sixteen-month-old toddler, was very interested in watching the process.

The VPV salesman commented on how cute she was and asked if she was our only child. Unbeknownst to him, he had stumbled on a gold mine with that question.

Just a few days prior, I had given birth to our second child, a three-and-a-half-pound baby boy who had arrived eight weeks early. Our baby was still in intensive care, and we were dealing with the worry and stress of watching our tiny infant struggle for survival.

We told the VPV salesman about our son, thus arming him with the ammo he needed to close the deal. He offered us sympathy and demonstrated the wonder of the VPV on our old orange shag carpet. Having placed a black cloth over the intake hose, he quickly showed us how much dirt was picked up by the VPV.

I admitted that it had been awhile since I had vacuumed; I had just given birth a few days earlier, and I was never the world's most enthusiastic housekeeper, even when I wasn't post-partum. He asked if he could use the vacuum cleaner we currently owned to clean another area of the carpet.

Hey, free vacuuming! My husband got the vacuum out for him, and the VPV salesman vacuumed a different area of the carpet. When he was finished, he replaced his black cloth on the VPV with a clean black cloth and proceeded to vacuum over the area he had just "cleaned" with our vacuum cleaner.

He showed us the dirt that had collected on the black cloth and said, "Would you want your daughter playing on this floor? Or your new little baby crawling on it?"

He left that night with a signed contract at 24.99 percent APR for the VPV that cost three months' worth of rent. Recovering from childbirth as I was, I was unable to use our new VPV, but my husband was able to. He vacuumed the entire apartment, and I felt like I had done something to help my tiny newborn son.

Buyer's remorse set in about the time we had to make payments on the VPV. I also realized that it was one of the heaviest vacuum cleaners I had ever used. It sure could suck up the dirt, though. My daughter loved sitting on it, backwards, while I vacuumed. She would hold on to the handle and grin the whole time I strained to use it.

I also learned not to judge my own mother so harshly. You see, when I was about ten years old, a vacuum cleaner sales-man stopped by our house. He wasn't selling the VPV—he was selling a VPVWW (Very Powerful Vacuum cleaner

With Water). The truly amazing thing about my mother pur-
chasing the VPVWW was that we didn't even have carpet in
our house.

I think one of the fantastic abilities the VPVWW had
was that it could even clean drapes! Of course, we didn't have
drapes, either; we had plastic curtains. But if we had ever had
carpet or drapes, the VPVWW would have done an amazing
job on both of them. Instead we used it mainly as an electric
broom, and then whined when we had to empty the sludge out
of the water basin.

We are all vulnerable to Vacuum Cleaner Salesmen at
some time in our lives. It may not be a vacuum cleaner; it could
be a time-share condo (that's another story for another day) or
a security system for our home (yet another tale).

The things I think I learned from these vulnerabilities
are:

1) you can learn from your mistakes, or
2) you can keep repeating them.

When the old VPV died and went to vacuum cleaner
heaven, we vowed we would never be "sucked" into a pricey
vacuum cleaner again. We haven't been (yet), although I did
re-carpet a couple of rooms to get a "free" vacuum cleaner—
and it doesn't even clean the drapes!

**eeds . . .**

*W . . . W . . . W
When I whine indeed,
I wander forth to find,
That a neighbor's pulled my weeds*

One day, a neighbor stopped me in the hallway at church and demanded to know how my husband did it. "Did what?" I asked, clueless as to what he was talking about.

"I drove by your house yesterday," he explained. "There you were, mowing the lawn while your husband was playing basketball in the driveway with your sons. I'd like to know how your husband trained you to do that."

This fellow was deflated when I told him no amount of training worked on me—I mowed the lawn because I enjoyed it. I liked mowing much better than playing basketball with my sons (or daughters), which, as you'll recall, had resulted in my breaking my nose on one occasion.

I willingly mowed the lawn until my children wanted to earn extra money and the mowing was starting to result in too much back pain for me. Then the time came when we couldn't afford to pay my children for mowing, so they had to rotate through taking turns with the lawns. My motherly guilt, combined with my desire to work in the yard and sunshine, resulted in me volunteering to do the weeding.

This worked pretty well until I realized how quickly my back began hurting when I weeded. Then I calculated how much I would actually accomplish in the twenty minutes I could manage to weed two or three times a week. I multiplied this by my yard's two-hundred-foot by four-foot weed-filled dirt edge. It didn't take me long to figure out I was fighting a losing battle.

The weeds grew faster than the pile of empty food wrappers in my teenage son's room, faster than the mound of dishes that filled the sink before I finished putting the clean ones away, and even faster than the pink cat ring that surrounded my shower and tub when I neglected to clean them.

I have developed a pattern of dealing with these issues: I ignore them. This strategy works until the problem grows so big you can no longer ignore it because it actually blocks your way.

I realized the weeds had hedged up my way when we got home from a week-long trip. Someone must have fed those weeds Miracle-Gro while we were gone because some of them were as tall as I was! That's an actual fact, no dramatization added.

I tried to rationalize that one woman's weed was another's attractive landscaping. After reading a question in a magazine that argued this very point, I was amazed to learn that a weed by any other name is still a weed. Some are noxious. Mine were just obnoxious.

At this point I was literally "faced" with the weeds in my yard, and I'll admit to being embarrassed by how terrible the problem was.

Whenever I realize how bad something like this has gotten I handle my embarrassment by doing the logical thing—I announce the situation to all who will listen (and to some who probably don't).

It's like seeing yourself in a photograph and realizing how chunky you've really become. The next thing you do is go around telling everyone you see that you need to lose ten or twenty pounds, as if they haven't realized it long before you admitted it to yourself.

So I told several of my neighbors about the extreme weed growth in my yard. In an attempt to excuse my neglectful behavior, I also reminded them of my fibromyalgia and how much it hurt my back to weed. I bemoaned the fact that I just couldn't keep up.

In my defense, I did this to cover my embarrassment over the shabby appearance of my yard. In my husband's defense, I didn't say anything to him about my yard mortification. I think the weeds were still invisible to him because they hadn't yet grown quite as tall as he was.

I forgot about broadcasting my weed woes to my friends until a couple of mornings later when I went outside and noticed a patch of weeds had been completely eradicated—torn out by their massive roots. This removal had not occurred by way of any of my family members—I could tell by the thoroughness of the job.

The dark, newly-turned patch of earth stood in stark

contrast to the rest of the perimeter. After admiring how absolutely wonderful that clean spot looked, my embarrassment turned to humiliation as I realized some anonymous weed-puller had graced a patch of my ground. I told my husband of the good deed done to us, and he shook his head. In his mind, I deserved to be embarrassed.

I was very grateful to the person(s) unknown who had performed the act of service. I knew first-hand what hard work it was, but I kind of wished they'd done the entire thing. Nothing makes a slob look sloppier than a neat freak next to her. In my mind, I narrowed it down to one or two likely per-petrators. They were both extremely busy people, yet they had made time to help me. Interestingly enough, they never came back to finish the job. I hope my weeds didn't completely deter them from helping others.

Motivated by guilt and a desire to continue the good, clean start I'd been given, I proceeded to work on the yard a little each day. My husband joined in as well, probably to keep me from begging for more anonymous help. He would have done it sooner if I had asked instead of hinted. I later hinted that he should have done it without being asked, but I don't think he took that hint, either.

So my yard finally got weeded just in time to start the whole process over again. The following year, my husband made a pre-emptive strike with a gallon of Round-up and a sprayer. Unfortunately, the spray took out four of our eleven perimeter bushes.

That was no tragedy, in my opinion, as the bushes were quite ugly and served no good purpose other than providing an eighteen-inch circumference that overshadowed all weeds, except for the morning glory.

That summer the weeds were under control, but the blight on our front yard took the form of four dry, brown, dead bushes amidst seven ugly, green, healthy ones. I planted petunias, but since the bushes were about three feet tall, the flowers didn't camouflage the dead bushes very well.

A turning point came when my thirteen-year-old, slightly pyro-maniacal son lit some fireworks in the cul-de-sac in front of our house. He had permission to do so, but a fire-blooming ground flower skipped over the curb and landed in a dead shrub. Whoosh! Just like that, we had a burning bush episode in our front yard.

Fortunately, my son remembered fire-safety training and sent his friend in to alert me as he turned the hose on the flames. I stood in horror, phone in hand, watching the breeze blow the flame toward the next dead shrub. My son kept spraying the fiery bush, and before I could ask the number to 9-1-1, he was able to douse the inferno, preventing any of the other bushes from bursting into flames.

That evening, my husband and son ripped the rest of the bushes out by their roots with the help of a tow chain and our Suburban. The gaping holes were soon filled in, and only two or three petunias died. The rest of the flowers were so glad to be in the sun they burst forth in full-bloom. Alas, so did the weeds.

I have never purposely watered the weeds, yet they grow and grow. On the other hand, I have deliberately watered my houseplants (at least once a month) yet they die, one by one. Why is this?

I may have hit on a solution. Perhaps I should bring the weeds inside my house and transplant my house plants outside. Or, I could just announce the whole thing to my friends and see what happens.

-ray . . .

X is quite exceptional,
For example, see X-ray,
When you can't see deeply on your own,
Expectations block your way.

When my mother was receiving her diagnosis and treatment for cancer, she spent many days in the hospital. My relationship with my mother was never a close one—maybe she was overwhelmed by six unruly children, perhaps I judged her too harshly because of her codependent personality (although I didn't recognize it at the time), or it could be I was too immature to nurture what basic relationship did exist.

I moved out of my mother's home when I was fourteen and she married her third husband; in my opinion, he was the worst of the trio. I lived with an older married sister for a couple of years, and then moved on to live with a family that had taken in my other sister. I only saw my mother a few times a year after that and spoke to her on the telephone only occasionally.

One time, when her current husband had been out of work for several years, he purchased a "leisure suit" at the local thrift store. I commented to my mother that it was just as well—he had no use for working clothes.

The diagnosis of cancer came after she completed a whirlwind tour of the eastern U.S. with her third husband, my two younger brothers, and a stolen Diner's Club card.

Terminal illness has a way of overcoming some family pettiness, so thankfully we tried to put aside our differences during the time we had left to spend with her. One afternoon we were visiting with my mother while she was in the hospital. She was telling us about various x-rays and CT-scans she had undergone.

"I had to get a CT-scan of my head this morning. They had to check my brain," she told us matter-of-factly.

Knowing that the medical staff was trying to determine just how far the cancer had spread, we were anxious to hear the results. I asked her, "What did they find?"

"Not a darn thing!" she exclaimed—only she didn't say darn. She laughed at her joke and we felt relief that she could laugh at such a difficult time.

Within a few short months of her diagnosis, she passed away. I was twenty-two at the time and had not lived with her for eight years, so I felt somewhat emotionally distant.

I felt that her lifestyle choices had distanced me from her while she was living, and unfortunately, I had dwelt on the negative aspects of our relationship for so long that the chasm grew wide. When I attended her funeral, I was surprised by how little I knew her. The recurrent message at her funeral was, "She never lost her sense of humor."

I filed the information away in my youthful, selfish brain.

As the years passed, I didn't think of my mother much, and when I did, it was usually disparagingly. I concentrated on not repeating her mistakes, or on proving I was different than my parental heritage (my father had been an absentee parent since I was three, and prior to that had been absent due to incarceration).

I spoke little about my mother and even less about my father. My own children grew up with only one grandparent—my husband's father had passed away prior to our marriage. That seemed normal to them.

I found that as I struggled with parenthood, I slowly came to realize that the choices you make as a parent aren't always black and white. You make the best decision you can, only to have hindsight reveal a better solution. As I progressed in my maturity (a euphemism for "got older"), I regretted my inability to get past all the emotional baggage before my mother died. I realized that since she was gone and her parents were gone, I could not get answers to questions that suddenly started to form in my mind.

Sometimes I felt sorry for myself; most of the time I pushed it away. I was what I was—I didn't have a living mother, the relationship we had while was alive was unsatisfactory, and I hadn't wanted most of what she had to offer me anyway.

Then I became aware of something interesting happening. I can best share it with a few examples. I would call my children to dinner with the same song my mother used to sing out, "Come and get it while it's hot, festered eyeballs fried in snot!" My children would go "Eeeeeew! Did you make that up? Sick!" I admitted my mother used to say it.

I would tell them that I was busier than a "one-legged man in a butt-kicking contest"—another echo of my mother. I described a shopping trip with my daughter (who loves to shop, whereas I despise it) as being drug "all over heck and half of Georgia!" Again, courtesy of my mother, —only she didn't say heck.

I quipped that I would do a certain thing if "the good Lord was willing and the devil don't object"—my mother's words. A slick surface was described as "slicker than snot on a doorknob." When asked where I was going, I would say "to Hades and back to see how far it is"—only my mom didn't say Hades.

My daughter pointed out one day that my mom said some really funny things. I had a flashback to the funeral when people said, "She never lost her sense of humor." I realized they were right; not only did she never lose her sense of humor, she actually had one in the first place! This was a revelation to me!

For the first time that I can remember, I felt pride in my parentage—at least on my mother's side. I honestly don't know enough about my father's side to comment intelligently.

But I was blessed with a sense of humor—albeit a sometimes twisted, sick sort of humor. As I observed my siblings with their surprisingly dry wit, I realized we had inherited something from our mother—something good. We had the ability to laugh and find humor in almost any situation. That is a gift to treasure.

What has any of this to do with x-rays? Just as an x-ray clears away the obstacles so the bones or internal organs can be viewed unobstructed, we sometimes need the obstacles cleared away so we can see what really lies beneath.

In my case, it took years to realize that something really good was under all the stuff I considered bad. I had taught my children for years and years to look beneath the surface, but I had a tough time practicing what I preached.

What I learned? Look deeper. Unless you're looking at the baseboards of my house or the grime on my windows, that is. If you look too closely there, you may think my house was "going to heck in a hand basket," only you wouldn't say heck.

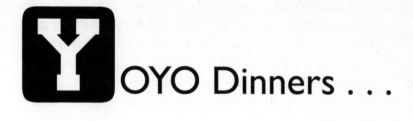

YOYO Dinners . . .

Big Y, Little Y,
Youngsters yell and yearn,
"You're On Your Own" for dinner,
I hope yours doesn't burn.

I mentioned earlier how we assigned dinner nights to each of the children. That worked pretty well and took care of four nights of the week, since we implemented it when only four of our children were still at home.

That still left three other nights for me to decide what to fix for dinner—Friday, Saturday, and Sunday. Sundays were easy. We had a standard Sunday dinner of roast beast, mashed potatoes and gravy, rolls, and a vegetable. That happened to be my husband's favorite meal.

Since pizza is my favorite food (chocolate excluded), Fridays were usually pizza night. That left Saturday. I could usually rely on a Saturday night date with my husband and it usually involved dinner. I loved going out to dinner with just the two of us, but I had one problem with it—I thought it was wrong to expect me to cook for the children before I went out to eat, and I felt guilty making them go hungry.

I determined it wouldn't work to make one of the children cook for the others since they can be pretty mean to each other when they choose to be. I tried to ignore the issue of dinner for the kids and let them figure it out, but too many times I would come home from my dinner out with my husband to the wretched little creatures looking hopeful that I had brought them a morsel.

We toyed with the idea of not having pizza on Friday and ordering it for them on Saturday before we went out, but I didn't want to miss out on pizza. I wanted to have my pizza and eat out too!

So we devised the plan of every child for himself. It was not a new plan, but it was a plan. We had to actually tell them the plan though, so they wouldn't conveniently forget to eat dinner until it was time to go to bed.

We called this the YOYO dinner—meaning You're On Your Own. It meant each child was required to fix and eat his or her own dinner. They could choose what they wanted, as long as they could fix it themselves and the main ingredient wasn't sugar or chocolate.

It was liberating. I didn't feel obligated to cook for them, and they were excited to choose what they wanted. YOYO worked especially well for them when I went on date nights with my husband.

As time passed and I stopped working outside the home, I had more time and desire to cook, and the nights of each child picking a dinner menu faded into the past. Once again, I was in charge of deciding what was for dinner.

Any stay-at-home mom can testify that just because you

don't work outside the home, it doesn't mean you don't work. The focus shifts from working for your employer to working for your family, and your family is usually reluctant to fork over a paycheck to you twice a month for your efforts on their behalf.

I found I was working just as hard, but on different things. Our three oldest children had the ability to come home from school, get started on their homework, and get it completed, usually before I came home from work. Our three youngest children are more athletically than academically inclined, so they needed much more hands-on help with homework.

The result was that some days I was just as tired from being a homemaker as I was when I held down a full-time job as a CFO. Even though I had learned to enjoy cooking more, I had a more limited budget to work with, so the weekly dinners out and weekly or semiweekly pizza had to stop.

We were still picky eaters, and we got sick of having the same menus over and over, I found that our YOYO dinners came in handy again. Now it wasn't just for date night; it was also for running-kids-to-all-their-different-activities night, for I-forgot-to-go-to-the-store night, for I-just-can't-think-of-anything-for-dinner night, and for any other night I just couldn't muster up the gumption to cook.

Then my children caught on. Whenever they were experiencing an I-don't-like-what's-for-dinner night they would ask if they could YOYO. We ended up with more YOYOs than a toy store. I couldn't prepare the correct amount of food for any dinner, because someone was always trying to YOYO. Soon I had to put a screeching halt to the anarchy.

So, like many great ideas, the YOYO dinner worked—in moderation and under careful parental supervision. It just turns out that I'm the parent that needs to be supervised. At least my children know how to do a little cooking now.

Zoomph . . .

Big Z, Little Z,
What begins with Z?
I do! You can call me Zoomph,
Whether I'm a he or she.

Every few years, I get hit by a creative fit and decide to make handmade presents for Christmas gifts. One year I crocheted lovely clothes hangers, which would have been quite useless and limp if they had not already contained a handy wooden hanger in the center. I crocheted some frilly pink and white carnations that never need water or grow weeds—although dusting them is another matter.

Different craft fads come and go. One time, I made journals for each of my children. These consisted of binders covered with batting and fabric. On the front of each, I framed a cute little picture of the child to whom the book was given. I filled them with paper and encouraged each child to start writing regularly.

My youngest child at the time was just learning to read and write. He liked the idea of keeping a journal, especially when he saw his older brother and sister doing so.

Because he wasn't content with just drawing pictures in the book, I offered to write his thoughts down for him.

He had me write a few simple sentences describing his day. It went something like, "I am in school. I like to play. I rode my bike today with a helmet and pants." It was generic and largely forgettable, until he added a sentence that has stuck with me for at least fifteen years.

He dictated, "When I grow up I want to name my child Zoomph."

My pen stopped mid-sentence. "Zoomph?" I questioned. "Zoomph," he confirmed.

I asked him if it was a boy's name or a girl's name. He said it didn't matter—Zoomph was the name he wanted. I asked him what would happen if his future wife didn't like the name. He assured me she would.

It was a name I'd never heard before or since, except when I've repeated it. And repeat it, I have. It's one of those things you never let your child forget. Through the years I've been able to keep reminding him of the name he has picked out for his firstborn. He gets irritated and tells me to stop. I remind him that I am merely keeping his dream alive, the one I personally recorded for him.

Since he has matured (a little), he has admitted that he has no intention of naming his child Zoomph. I tell him, "That's okay. I'm still calling him Zoomph. Or her. It doesn't matter to me which it is."

He hasn't argued with me that it should be held in confidence, that he was dictating into his personal journal, and I should have forgotten what I transcribed. I don't think that would help, though. I can't seem to stop myself.

It seems I can't resist teasing, tormenting, and being just plain contrary to my children. When they ask for something perfectly reasonable, I say "no" as I nod my head. I tell them, "You get nothing," as I hand them what they are asking for.

Then I wonder why they don't take me seriously.

I take the words they say literally, even when I know they don't mean them that way. When they get a puzzled look on their faces, I explain how their words can be twisted. They are learning from a pro.

I told my youngest daughter that I was going to crawl into the bathtub to take a nice long bath. She was about six at the time and asked, "Are you literally going to crawl?" I looked at her in surprise, wondering if I'd heard her correctly. She was making crawling motions with her hands and said, "You know, crawl into the tub." Not only did she know how to say the word "literally," she knew what it meant.

Now back to the issue of names. My mother had six children whom she named Gary, Sherry, Carrie, Terri, Barry, and Jerry. Did I mention her name was Mary? Oh, yeah, Sherry married Harry (they later divorced).

I get a kick out of telling people the names of my siblings. Every now and then someone will ask, "Did your mother do that on purpose?" To which I always reply, "No. Isn't that amazing?" They usually start to nod their heads before they catch on. Sometimes it takes awhile because I'm able to say most things with a straight face.

I've done this for so long that I forget that I have a habit of saying the most outrageous things without smiling. I figure people have to know I'm kidding—after all, nobody would say things that are as bizarre as the things I say, unless they were joking or seriously lacking in social skills. Oh, wait—maybe I just need to develop some good manners.

When my children say strange things or come up with unique names for their children, I suppose they come by it naturally. When they twist my words or neglect to take me seriously because I'm always joking, I have no one to blame but myself. Nature or nurture—either way they're doomed.

In spite of my efforts to warp them, the rising generation looks pretty great to me. The generation beyond that—"Well, little Zoomph, I can't wait to meet you!"

About the Author

Terri Ferran was born in Virginia and grew up in a small Colorado town that you could easily miss if you blinked while driving through it. As she got older, she realized people were constantly blinking, and she, herself, had already blinked a good portion of her life away. She ventured a few hundred miles away to the big city, where she met her husband. They currently reside in the beautiful Rocky Mountains.

Although she always dreamed of becoming a writer, Terri followed the secure career of accounting, which she hoped would always provide her with the luxuries she craved—living indoors and eating regularly. She is a CPA who spent many years in public accounting and as the CFO of an automotive dealership group.

Having very nearly lost her sense of humor along the way, she finally got brave enough to quit working in the safe world of numbers to pursue her dream of writing and to spend more time with her children.

Terri is the author of two successful inspirational novels, but this is her first foray into non-fiction. She has done her best to tell the truth and limit the exaggerations to her works of fiction.

Terri and her husband are the parents of six children—three boys and three girls. When she's not busy writing or doing mom things, Terri still loves to read, but can usually be found doing laundry or dishes, running errands, napping, eating chocolate, or exercising (not necessarily in that order).

Acknowledgments

I would like to thank my children, to whom this book is dedicated, for providing so much fodder for my writing, even if some of them refuse to read it.

To my sisters-not-by-blood, Melissa Catmull, Mindi Faulkner, and Michelle Ferran, who are always willing to read the drafts—however rough they may be. Thanks!

I'm indebted to my sister, Carrie Lew, for helping me remember things I'd sometimes rather forget!

My mother-in-law, Susan Crawford gets a shout-out for several things—producing awesome children, encouraging my writing, and eagerly asking to read whatever I write. She even makes her husband, John, read the stuff too.

A special acknowledgment goes to Julie Turnbow, my kindred spirit friend, and Trisha Tracy, my back-yard neighbor, for being "first readers." They are always excited about and supportive of all my writing endeavors—or at least they put on good acts.

Finally, and eternally, I want to express gratitude to my husband, Jose Isauro Ramon Ferran III—Tod, for short—for being the first and last sounding board for this book and all the other random thoughts that pop into my head.